When the Body Speaks Its Mind

When the Body Speaks Its Mind

. . .

A Psychiatrist Probes the Mysteries of
Hypochondria and Munchausen's Syndrome

BERNEY GOODMAN, M.D.

A Jeremy P. Tarcher/Putnam Book
published by
G. P. Putnam's Sons
New York

A Jeremy P. Tarcher/Putnam Book
Published by G. P. Putnam's Sons
Publishers Since 1838
200 Madison Avenue
New York, NY 10016

CONFIDENTIALITY

In order to protect the privacy of my patients, all names, physical descriptions, biographical details, and identifiable events have been changed. I have followed the guidelines set down in the *Opinions of the Ethics Committee on Principles of Medical Ethics,* published by the American Psychiatric Association in 1989. Any similarity to real individuals or places arises from the commonality of experiences of people who suffer from emotional illness.

Requests for such permissions should be addressed to:
Jeremy P. Tarcher, Inc.
5858 Wilshire Blvd., Suite 200
Los Angeles, CA 90036

Library of Congress Cataloging-in-Publication Data

Goodman, Berney
When the body speaks its mind / Berney Goodman.
p. cm.
A psychiatrist probes the mysteries of hypochondria and Munchausen's syndrome.
Includes bibliographical references and index.
ISBN 0-87477-758-5 (acid-free paper)
1. Somatization disorder.   2. Somatization disorder—Case studies.
3. Hypochondria.   4. Munchausen syndrome.   I. Title.
RC552.S66G66   1994
616.85'2—dc20   93-28894 CIP

Printed in the United States of America
1   2   3   4   5   6   7   8   9   10

This book is printed on acid-free paper.
∞

To Irene, my everything

Contents

ACKNOWLEDGMENTS

Dr. Hillel Swiller, friend and esteemed colleague, inspired me to write this book. He suggested I put in writing what I had previously only spoken at innumerable teaching conferences. When his advice proved insufficient to make me jump on board, he further ventured that I had a talent for storytelling. I am forever grateful to him for so insightfully recognizing my susceptibilities and launching me on what has turned out to be a joyous voyage of exploration and discovery.

The trip has not been without its storms, and George Ryan has helped me navigate through many of them with supportive and constructive advice. He never lost faith in me or the project.

My editor, Susan Leon, brought the manuscript (and me) down to size and skillfully illuminated the principle "less is more."

I want to thank Lucy Schmolka, who set me on the trail of one of the Munchuasen histories.

My patients made this book possible. Over the years they confirmed that my choice of profession was a correct one by making each day interesting and new. Although I have disguised their identities to preserve their privacy, I hope I have accurately portrayed their humanness, their fears, struggles, hopes, disappointments, and triumphs.

My children Alexis, Lowell, and Lawrence, fine writers all, provided a standard I could only hope to match.

But it is my wife, Irene, who deserves most of my gratitude. She not only put my primitive attempts at writing into English, she also suffered the brunt of all the stress writing provoked in me. It is a testament to her love and devotion that not once during the writing process did I express my vast emotional discomfort through physical symptoms.

Introduction

The chief of neurology was a brilliant, revered, but somewhat gruff man in his sixties. I was one of his assistants. One day, a young man, a psychiatrist in his early thirties, was on the neurologist's private patient roster. He entered the office accompanied by his pregnant wife. He claimed he had the symptoms of a dread disease, amyotrophic lateral sclerosis, or Lou Gehrig's disease. This is a slow, but progressive, degeneration of the nervous system that leads to paralysis and an agonizing death.

Today's patient had, for some months, been observing twitching in the muscles of his legs and ripples of muscular activity cascading down his calves. At first, he tried to ignore these twitches. In time, they increased in frequency and could not be overlooked. The psychiatrist knew about Lou Gehrig's disease and that it usually struck much older people. Nonetheless, he had begun to fear that he was becoming one of its youthful victims.

The famed neurologist listened intently and seemed, for the moment, to suspend his gruffness. He continued to be kind while proceeding with his customary thorough neurological examination. Then, abruptly, he exclaimed in a loud and disagreeable tone, "There's nothing wrong with you. Get out of here."

As the couple left, the neurologist mumbled a snide remark about "crazy" psychiatrists. For him it was, undoubtedly, another case brought to an efficient conclusion. But although I, too, could close the case when it came to excluding a diagnosis of Lou Gehrig's disease, I could not get this patient out of my mind and I began to speculate on the implications of this psychiatrist-patient's problems. If his muscular twitches had no medical cause, did they have a psychological one? If so, what was going on in his head that resulted in those alarming twitches? It took awhile before I arrived at a picture of what might have transpired in that psychiatrist-patient's mind and how it was translated into *fear of a fatal illness.*

The prospective father, like so many before him, had been under a particular stress: the anticipation of a first child. Until his wife's pregnancy, he must have been the exclusive beneficiary of her care, attention, and love. Now he was to share it with another—the child who was twitching and kicking in his wife's womb. The psychiatrist must have often put his hand on her growing belly and felt those sensations of new life. He certainly must have expressed his joy to his wife and others, but down deep might there have been suppressed negative feelings that the psychiatrist was now expressing, not in words, but in physical language? The rippling of his leg muscles could be his way of saying, "I am just as important as that other twitcher who is about to replace me as the king of my castle and whose intrusion I resent."

This explanation may sound glib and crudely Freudian—a young psychiatrist's speculations and ruminations, unfounded and unsupported by evidence. Perhaps. But I had a distinct advantage when I formulated this theory. As you may have guessed, I was both the observer and the patient.

That experience in the neurologist's office and my attempts to clarify my thoughts about it profoundly affected both my professional and personal life. Professionally, I developed a lifelong interest in *somatization,* a process through which people express emotional discomfort in a physical rather than verbal language. Instead of words, this language consists of unwelcome physical sensations, physical symptoms, and preoccupations with having medical illness. For example, after a grueling day at the office or an argument with a spouse or child, a headache or a stiff neck may express our feelings.

Somatization is a way of saying "I am emotionally over-whelmed." In place of putting a feeling of emotional discomfort into words such as "I'm feeling anxious because . . ." or "I feel under the weather because . . . ," we communicate through phys-ical discomfort or symptoms or worry about sickness. It is a common language, used by almost all of us at one time or an-other. Somatization symptoms are not part of the imagination and are never feigned. They are genuinely, and often painfully, experienced.

From a personal point of view, it was sobering to realize that, despite my being a psychiatrist, I was just as susceptible as the next person to expressing my emotional discomfort with physical symptoms. In fact, 60 to 80 percent of Americans have at least one somatization symptom per week. Research has provided powerful evidence that most of us express emotional discomfort physically far more often than verbally.

Indeed, we all experience occurrences of somatization, whether or not we are aware of them. For the most part, these are related to stress and are normal. We usually identify the physical feel-ings as stress-induced and may say, "I had such a bad day at the office, my stomach is still tied up in knots," or "I'm tense—I feel it in my neck." These sensations are usually relieved by a drink, nap, hot bath, good dinner, exercise, or a good night's sleep.

Similarly, when under pressure to complete a project, confront a new social situation, or start a new job, we may experience heartburn, palpitations, or urges to go to the bathroom fre-quently. In these forms of somatization, we are aware of the re-lationship between stress and our physical sensations and do not impart medical significance to them.

When we do associate an unwanted physical sensation with medical illness, we have developed a symptom.

A symptom is a body change that we subjectively perceive as a sign that we are sick. For instance, if I decide that my palpita-tions mean I have heart disease, my palpitations become a symp-tom. The onset of symptoms usually follows a pattern. Under stressful circumstances, which we may or may not be aware of, we may be prone to indigestion, nausea, lower-back pain, repeated urges to go to the bathroom, headaches, palpitations, or shortness of breath—to name a few of the more usual symptoms. We hope these will disappear, but they persist. Then, at some point, it strikes us forcibly, and alarmingly, that these changes must mean something is physically wrong. We visit a doctor. And most often, the physician, having taken a history and done some basic testing, reassures us that there is nothing physically wrong. We accept this opinion and, as the stress abates, the symptoms fade or disappear altogether. Like somatization without symptoms (where we do not interpret the physical discomfort as a sign of sickness), the presence of these symptoms does not mean we have serious emotional problems or emotional illness.

How can the doctor be sure there is *absolutely* nothing physically wrong? The fact that a physician cannot identify a medical condition does not mean that none exists. Indeed, certain illnesses are notoriously difficult to diagnose in their early stages, and doctors may lack the diagnostic skill to detect them. Generally speaking, however, when a thorough medical investigation continues to find no evidence of physical disease, a doctor can reasonably attribute the symptoms to somatization. In addition, most experienced physicians, particularly those who have a long acquaintance with their patients, recognize the contribution of stress and emotional difficulties to their patients' symptomatologies.

When the somatization symptoms persist despite a physician's reassurances and, more importantly, interfere with daily functioning, they require more serious attention. For instance, if we continue to complain of the same symptoms and consult many specialists, take days off from work, and preoccupy ourselves and our families with our complaints, we may indeed have an emotional disorder and require psychiatric diagnosis and treatment. Psychiatrists recognize an emotional condition as a disorder rather than just a problem when the psychological troubles begin to seriously affect a person's everyday functioning over an extended period of time. The dysfunction must represent a marked deviation from what is accepted as normal by any particular culture and is not merely an expected response to what is going on in someone's life. For example, there are people who cannot work, or have given up eating and lost fifty pounds but are not dieting, or have stopped talking, or are so anxious they cannot leave the house because of their emotional problems.

Thus we say that those who have persistent somatization symptoms that markedly interfere with their functioning have somatoform disorders. The commonest somatoform disorder is hypochondria. But isn't hypochondria what we have been talking about all along? Not as far as doctors, particularly psychiatrists, are concerned. Hypochondria is a particular variety of somatization in which the somatization symptoms have persisted for longer than six months and in which the person has unrealistic fears of disease. Producing marked effects on an individual's interpersonal relationships and performance at home and work, hypochondria can become a way of life for many.

Secondary hypochondria is the term used when the somatization symptoms are part of the symptomatology of other identifiable and treatable emotional disorders, such as depressive disorders, anxiety disorders, and panic disorder. Treating these disorders—with accurate diagnosis, medication, and psychotherapy—delivers a double bonus: both the emotional disorder symptoms and somatization symptoms can be relieved.

I am not talking here about psychosomatic illness. In psychosomatic illness, such as duodenal ulcer and ulcerative colitis, an identifiable physical illness is always present; the pathology is recognizable to the naked eye, through instruments, or through laboratory testing, or all three. In somatization, despite the reality of the pain that people feel, they have *no physical illness*.

Somatization also must not be confused with the intermittent worries about illness that we all have. Similarly, intense attention to particular bodily functions, such as inordinate attention to bowel habits, while common, is not somatization.

While intermittent forms of somatization may appear to be nothing more than a temporary inconvenience, their significance for our society as a whole goes way beyond this. First, because somatization is so widespread, we can read this as a barometer of how stressful life in our society has become. Second, people with somatization symptoms constitute a major public health-care problem, adding significantly to health-care costs because of the extensive and repetitive testing that they, their physicians, and their symptoms call for. A study done over ten years ago put the bill for physicians seeing people with somatization symptoms at $20 billion, or 10 percent of the nation's total annual health-care outlay. We can assume that this figure has matched the nation's rising health-care costs since then. And, depending on which figures you believe, between 20 and 84 percent of people who consult a doctor do so for some form of somatization. Hypochondria alone is said to be present in 9 percent of patients who consult their family physicians.

Although we can estimate its cost to the nation, somatization is not well understood or recognized. In fact, it is misunderstood. For example, a physician friend of long standing, whom I know to be quite emotionally stable, told me he recently had an MRI (magnetic resonance imaging) of his head. He said he had been experiencing a loss of sensation on the left side of his upper lip and feared there might be something neurologically wrong. Although the examining neurologist found nothing, he suggested an MRI just to play it safe. The results of the MRI confirmed the neurologist's original findings, and normal sensation quickly returned to my friend's upper lip. I suggested that he had had a somatization symptom, a response perhaps to some unrecognized stress in his life. I knew his wife had just returned to the workplace after years of staying home to raise their children. He did not comment.

When he had gone, my teenage daughter, who had heard our conversation, said, "How could you have said that to him? How could you have told him he was a somatizer? You should have seen his eyes when you said that. I just know what he was thinking—that you were saying he was crazy or something, or faking it."

Regardless of whether my daughter's observations were correct, she reminded me of the difficulties involved when you try to dislodge the belief that somatization—one of many expressions of mind/body interaction—constitutes certain evidence of deeply rooted emotional problems, mental disorder, or feigned illness.

Naturally, we are reluctant to associate ourselves with anything that fearful and embarrassing. It is difficult to alter such perceptions—even among members of my own family!

This book is intended to clarify somatization and the role the psychiatrist can play in its identification and treatment. In the first part, I try to show how, after years of misunderstanding, psychiatrists have sorted out the different types of somatization and organized them into a classification system that permits them and other physicians to communicate with one another and facilitate treatment of their patients. The terminology in this book, like the subject it describes, does not spring from my imagination. I owe much of the book's contents to the hundreds of psychiatrists and scientists who are devoted to mind/body research and have established a modern terminology to identify, understand, and explain concepts that have been confused up to now.

I think it is important to begin by dispelling some of the commonly held myths about psychiatry and its practitioners, and describing what it is we actually do to improve the quality of our patients' lives. From there, we explore the different forms of somatization and consider some theories of their origins.

In the patient stories of the book's second part, I hope to draw you into the psychiatrist's world and share cases I have seen and treated—some successfully, some less so. I hope to show that although the general concepts of somatization may be easily classified, somatization symptoms become unique when applied to the lives of individuals and the families, friends, and physicians they impact on. Only the stories of people who exhibit all somatization's varied forms can adequately illustrate its complex and complicated nature.

This book is about people—for the most part, ordinary people. Although they and some of their stories may seem bizarre and complex, they are only as bizarre and complex as the human condition. Additionally, understanding the severe and the abnormal can serve to clarify the mild and normal.

Along the way, you may be tempted to identify with various

elements of these patients' histories—to put yourself into the scenarios. You may even think you have the whole illness rather than a few shared features. You may even jump to the conclusion that you, too, have serious abnormalities. Don't worry. You are in good company. Just ask medical students about their initial reactions to the ill.

You may wish I had told you more about the patients I describe. Any sparseness of detail or unanswered questions about the emotional lives of these people is due as much to the brevity of some of my encounters as to the relative inability of somatizing patients to verbalize their emotions. It should come as no surprise that people who chronically reveal their emotional discomfort with physical symptoms are not usually in touch with their feelings and do not verbalize their emotions freely. Although the less than perfect outcomes and incomplete histories are due, in part, to the limitations of psychiatry and the patients themselves, I also assume full responsibility for my own shortcomings. I readily acknowledge that, in other hands, the outcomes may have been more favorable.

The third part of this book describes a rare condition, Munchausen syndrome, or factitious illness. This is somatization in its most extreme form, its victims coping with emotional distress by actually creating and feigning illnesses, often acute and rare, through self-mutilation, drug abuse, and a host of ruses—some clever, some not. They never stray far from physicians' offices or medical facilities and live much of their lives in hospitals. Once we define this illness, see some of the ways in which Munchausen syndrome patients afflict themselves, and consider some of the theories that attempt to explain this condition, I share some of the case histories that have baffled, saddened, and frustrated me and my colleagues.

In summary, this book is about my experiences over the years. What began as the visit of a distraught father-to-be to a knowing neurologist became an opportunity to integrate my training in both internal medicine and psychiatry, and galvanized my interest in the relationship between the mind and the body. The treatment of so many patients with mind/body problems and disorders has only made me more aware and convinced of the inseparability of the mind and body. We cannot compartmentalize peoples' prob-

lems as "physical" or "emotional," "medical" or "psychiatric."
They are all intertwined.

A psychiatrist finds gratification in helping others get on with
their lives, in easing distress and suffering. I have also enjoyed
sharing my experiences and insights with generations of students.
With this book, I have the chance to share them with you.

PART ONE

Somatization— When the Body Speaks Another Language

· 1 ·

The Psychiatrist as Detective

When I am asked, in social situations, what I do, and I answer that I am a psychiatrist, the questioners' responses tell me that they have, at best, a clouded understanding of my profession. More often than not, I am thought to be a clairvoyant with a medical diploma. All too often, I hear "Are you going to read my mind, Doc?" or "I'd better be careful of what I say—you're going to analyze me." The ostensibly more knowledgeable may ask, "Are you a Freudian or a Jungian?" The more au courant may say "Kleinian" or "Lacanian." Their good manners and fear of embarrassment relegate to silence other thoughts and fantasies.

In social situations, I have no interest in practicing or discussing psychoanalysis or any other psychiatric treatment. Instead, I listen politely. But I cannot help imagining comic-book scenes and empty dialogue clouds floating above the heads of those with whom I am conversing. I try to fill in the empty clouds with estimates of the speakers' unspoken perceptions of psychiatrists and psychiatry. Sometimes I conjure up an image of the nineteenth-century psychoanalyst, complete with Mittel Europa accent and Freud-like beard, sitting in a comfortable armchair behind a patient reclining on a couch. The patient is describing his childhood traumas or blaming his parents for his failings. The psychiatrist does not talk but takes copious notes.

Other images are darker. In these, members of my profession—myself included—are portrayed as eccentrics or nutty professors bent on exploiting their patients' weaknesses by twisting the meanings of their life stories and exaggerating the extent of their emotional problems. We are seen as delighting in labeling the normal abnormal and confining healthy individuals to filthy snakepits or cuckoo's nests. In another sequence, I see us rendering our patients drooling and brain damaged, having subjected them to allegedly mind-numbing shock treatments and lobotomies. Then there are the scenes in which we destroy minds with drugs that we prescribe to pacify troublemakers and turn dissidents into brainwashed tools of the state. Our preferred subjects are women, depicted as exploitable and helpless in a society dominated by men.

Sometimes I switch to another scenario in which the psychiatrist is a kind and sympathetic soul who listens raptly to the patient's travails and their origins in life's stresses and unfortunate circumstances. The psychiatrist says nothing until the very end of the recounting, and then the words that come—somehow miraculously—help the patient rise up off the couch ready to take on the harsh realities of the offensive and offending outside world. I am not quite sure how people think the psychiatrist accomplishes this. In the patient's mind, the practitioner who does this would probably have to assume the role of the perfect mother who demonstrates love with unmitigated support for the patient's ideas and wishes.

The mental game I play is unfair, of course. It is unreasonable to expect someone to understand the nature of another's work. However, it seems to me, the difficulty of understanding what a psychiatrist does is not just one of unfamiliarity, and I feel the public's perception of my profession is more distorted than its perception of other professions. I am sure people have a clearer idea of a cardiologist's or surgeon's work than of a psychiatrist's. Although I do spend much of my time listening to others, and sometimes I do sit behind them while my patients lie on my couch, and I do take notes and hear childhood memories, and I do like to think of myself as relatively benign and considerate, my job does not include any of the other activities I have portrayed.

What, then, do psychiatrists do? First and foremost, we are physicians, diagnosing and treating illnesses. Precisely, we are medical specialists, experts in the diagnosis and treatment of emotional problems and illnesses that express themselves with alterations of thoughts, emotions, and behavior. Note that I distinguish between illness and problems. This is important. We define illness as a condition marked by a pronounced deviation from a normal, healthy state. Illness involves symptoms and suffering that lead to a withdrawal from gratifying activities and active participation in society; in psychiatric parlance, this is called a disorder. Problems do not connote such severity.

We need also to distinguish between disease and illness. When disease is present, there are objective, measurable changes in the body. Disease and illness are usually found together, although disease can be present without illness, as in high blood pressure and early "silent" cancer. Similarly illness can be present without disease, as in somatization.

Emotional illness and problems are not the psychiatrist's only preoccupation; we are just as interested in mental health. We want to know which areas of emotional functioning work well and which areas do not. We want to know why one person enjoys mental health and why another has emotional problems or emotional illness. Although our specialty seems to abound with theories and schools of thought, our job as physicians is to arrive at a treatment plan for each patient based on an individual diagnosis. As with any physician, our task is to return the patient to a healthy state and make sure that status is maintained. We must do what is best for the patient.

Although psychiatrists have much in common with other physicians, we differ because we deal with subjective, emotion-based complaints that do not have observable features to verify them. For example, when making a diagnosis of heart failure, a cardiologist relies on a history of shortness of breath and swollen ankles and also observes the enlarged veins in the patient's neck, feels the abdomen for an enlarged liver, and then confirms these findings with a variety of laboratory tests and X-ray procedures. On the other hand, when making a diagnosis of depressive disorder, a psychiatrist depends on the accuracy of the patient's descriptions of thoughts and moods. This is the psychiatrist's examination. No sufficiently accurate lab tests or computerized scans exist to help the psychiatrist confirm the diagnosis of depression.

Misconceptions rooted in society's present and historical perceptions of mental health and illness contribute to the lack of understanding of the modern psychiatrist's work. Psychiatry has always walked a tightrope between the rational and the mystical, science and the soul. For at least two thousand years, psychiatrists have sought to explain and treat emotional problems rationally as illnesses with recognizable symptoms and specific treatments. They have always had to battle the concurrent and often more powerful views of magicians and shamans who too often have taken over the care of the mentally ill.

In nonpsychiatric medicine, the distinctions between normal and abnormal are quite straightforward and universally accepted. In psychiatry, the distinctions between normal and abnormal accepted as fairly standard by psychiatrists are often at odds with those of society. Normality can be defined as "agreeing with the regular and established type" and abnormality as "not normal—contrary to the usual structure, position, condition, behavior, or rule."

The way people's peers regard them is an important indicator of their normality, or lack of it. And the way peers regard the individual is determined, in large measure, by societal standards. Someone who is withdrawn, dresses bizarrely, and speaks in an odd tone of voice may be seen as an eccentric in an English pub but may be regarded as "sick" in New York. Through the ages, prophets have been venerated for their delusional thinking and hallucinatory experiences.

Over the centuries, as new concepts related to the working of the mind emerged and new treatments evolved, psychiatric terminology underwent many changes in attempts to clarify clouded perceptions. Instead of illumination, however, the results have often been distortion and pejorative use. The term *neurotic* is an example of how the meaning of a psychiatric term can be twisted and misused. In everyday usage, *neurotic* is a catchall term, often pejorative, that signifies an exaggerated, unanticipated, and illogical response in words or emotions. For psychiatrists, *neurotic* is also a catchall term, applying to a maladaptive way of dealing with anxiety or internal conflict, short of psychosis. Psychosis is a major mental disorder that grossly interferes with the interpretation of reality and the capacity to meet the ordinary demands of life. Later we will see how hypochondria has suffered the same misinterpretations and misapplications.

The metamorphosis of psychiatric terminology into indiscriminately used jargon—we easily call people paranoid, delusional, or hysterical—has made many people reluctant to consult psychiatrists for fear of being labeled. And when they do visit a psychiatrist, they are often much less forthcoming than they are with their other physicians. This makes the gathering of a psychiatric history more complicated than the taking of a medical history, although neither is easy.

The public's perceptions of psychiatrists and psychiatric patients also make psychiatric treatment more difficult. Many believe that psychiatric problems and even illness can be overcome through sheer dint of willpower. For these, treatment is a sign of weakness; it is more important that they take care of their problems on their own. Sometimes they succeed, not necessarily because they have willed the problems or illness away but because many psychiatric problems and disorders are self-limiting and do resolve themselves in time.

Those who do see psychiatrists almost always show some resistance to our recommendations. Although new medicines have revolutionized the field with their potential for improving a patient's quality of life in the short and long term, patients will accept any other specialist's prescriptions with fewer reservations and more hope than they will a psychiatrist's.

The psychiatric patient is reluctant to give the same straightforward answers he might provide to his family physician or another specialist. In fact, a patient's initial meetings with a psychiatrist often bristle with tension stemming from the patient's fear of being "caught." Relaxed and open with the nonpsychiatric physician, the same patient becomes defensive in the presence of the psychiatrist. These excerpts from rather typical doctor-patient encounters illustrate this point.

NONPSYCHIATRIC PHYSICIAN: How is your appetite?
PATIENT: Not so good lately, Doctor. It's off.

PSYCHIATRIST: How is your appetite?
SAME PATIENT: How would your appetite be if you had to
            eat this food?

For another straightforward question, the answers might be as
follows.

NONPSYCHIATRIC PHYSICIAN: How are you sleeping?
PATIENT: I wanted to tell you about that, Doctor. It's not
        what it used to be. I don't seem to be able to sleep
        through the night.

PSYCHIATRIST: How are you sleeping?
SAME PATIENT: There's so much noise here. How can I be expected
        to sleep? Would you be able to sleep with all of
        this going on?

The answers the psychiatrist gets suggest that the patient is thinking: I can't share the truth with him. He will find a hidden meaning in my answers. He may, in fact, exaggerate the importance of
my symptoms and label me "crazy."

Patients are often ashamed of their symptoms. For example,
most find it difficult to talk about their sexual lives. The psychiatrist asks, "How's your sex life?" and the patient answers almost automatically, "Just fine." This quick retort often proves to
be inaccurate.

Although people often fear medical illness, they do consult
doctors and are eager to share as much information as possible
because they believe this will help their physicians help them.
This is not always the case when the physician is a psychiatrist.
For instance, when I asked, "When you can't sleep at night, what
do you think about?" one patient answered, "I really don't think.
I feel like I have things on my mind. Like yesterday, I felt like
ugh. I don't want to think about it. I feel I'm getting into things
I don't understand, and I feel I'm not knowledgeable about it. I
don't understand it. I don't know what to think." I later learned
that this patient was preoccupied with fears of losing her mind.

If she expressed these fears openly, she ran the risk that I might confirm her suspicions.

Psychiatrists have to interpret information at quite a different level than nonpsychiatric physicians. They cannot simply accept what patients tell them at face value if they want to get to the heart of the matter and make an accurate diagnosis. But the psychiatrists must proceed cautiously and slowly. If they share their understanding of the underlying message of their patients' words, or ask questions that imply their understanding, they risk adding to the perception that they are mind readers and, true to stereotype, really are exaggerating the significance of what they are being told. Many patients are frightened when psychiatrists arrive at accurate diagnoses quickly, although they breathe sighs of relief when an internist or surgeon does so.

Apart from their conscious resistance to responding directly and forthrightly to a psychiatrist's questions, patients may not be aware of the answers. While some who see a psychiatrist may have direct access to their symptoms and are able to describe them accurately and with ease, more often than not, most patients experience and talk about their symptoms in vague terms. This may be because patients have relegated these thoughts to the unconscious and are not aware of them. We do this because these thoughts are unwanted or painful or because we may not have the capacity to understand them in psychological terms. Feelings of guilt also may crimp our ability to express ourselves openly and freely.

Psychiatrists thus have to develop interviewing techniques that circumvent these obstacles. They must learn how to ask questions in an indirect way, because direct questioning (the "Where does it hurt?" method of the nonpsychiatric physician) may hinder rather than help the free flow of information. Questions have to be paced, and psychiatrists need to be sufficiently sensitive to know when to press a point and when to leave it and wait until another opportunity arises. Psychiatrists learn when to infer other meanings from the information the patient offers. Psychiatrists learn not to talk much—and to choose their words carefully when they do. They are circumspect, interjecting statements and questions that make it easier for the patient to share material that is difficult and frightening.

The assessment of symptoms helps the psychiatrist to make a diagnosis, just as the detective draws his conclusions by analyzing the clues at hand. A patient told me, "I have these thoughts, Doctor. They come all the time. I suddenly think I want to expose myself, take my penis out, right there on the street. I don't want these thoughts." Here the patient has a symptom that he himself perceives as abnormal and unwanted, and the psychiatrist can make a diagnosis of obsessive thoughts.

Similarly, a patient is describing a set of symptoms when he says "I can't ride in elevators, and I am desperate because I am sometimes forced to climb thirty-two floors to get to work," or "I've spent twelve years trying to get this doctorate degree. Each time I come close to finishing my thesis, I collapse with anxiety and stay away from the computer for months."

The problem posed by many other patients is that they deny their symptoms. They rationalize their behavior and feelings as responses to external pressures of the norms and habits of the societies in which they live. The following conversation illustrates this point.

> PATIENT: I stay at home. I don't go out at all. I never used to stay home. I went out all the time.
> PSYCHIATRIST: You *never* go out?
> PATIENT: I have not been out of the house in six months.
> PSYCHIATRIST: Is there something you are afraid of?
> PATIENT: I have no fears. My mother is ill. I have to stay with her all the time. What kind of daughter would I be if I didn't?

Because those who see psychiatrists do not always specify their symptoms, even when they are clearly present, psychiatrists must find other means of assessing any abnormality or emotional disorder. To do this, the psychiatrist relies on estimates of the patient's day-to-day functioning. Sometimes the diminished functioning has always been present. At other times, functioning changes with the onset of emotional illness and becomes an indicator.

Accurate estimates of functioning require comparison to what other people of the patient's gender, age, and culture do under similar circumstance. For example, patterns of eating, sleeping, sexual activity, and relationships among children, parents, and siblings vary within cultures. But most people would agree that the woman who did not leave her house for six months was showing a change and diminution in functioning. The once-retiring man who suddenly becomes the life of the party and engages in indiscriminate sex is showing a change in functioning, although he may enjoy his new state and not complain of symptoms. The middle-aged woman who has never left her parents' home or shown any signs of independent thought or activity, choosing even to work in the family store, has had a chronic diminution of function, although again she may be asymptomatic. The woman living in a safe suburb who has had steel bars riveted to her doors and windows and lets no one into the house without first taking elaborate security precautions has not enjoyed full functioning, although she probably does not complain of symptoms and may even think her behavior is justified in this perilous modern world. In other societies, however, her behavior might be taken as normal. In Russia, padded double doors on apartments survive as remnants of an ever-prying communist regime.

A psychiatrist's nearest equivalent to a stethoscope is his awareness of his own emotional responses to his patients and his understanding of what his patients have done to elicit these reactions. This is one of his most important tools of evaluation and diagnosis. It distinguishes psychiatrists from nonpsychiatric physicians, who require no similar sensitivity.

The image of the modern psychiatrist I would like to share is that of the psychiatrist as detective, with the illness as the culprit. The psychiatrist is always searching for clues, listening to and beyond what the patient is saying, and paying attention to the smallest details.

As I have explored the workings of the mind, particularly in regard to the mind/body problems that are the focus of this book, I have often allowed myself to identify with Sherlock Holmes. Indeed the great sleuth's creator, Arthur Conan Doyle, was a physician as well as an author. He was a student of Joseph Bell, the famous Edinburgh surgeon who gave his name to Bell's palsy. Doyle is said to have been so impressed by Bell that he modeled Holmes after him.

Bell was renowned for being able to describe a person's life in detail after only a few seconds of observation. On one occasion, standing before a group of students in frock coat and striped pants, he described a new patient after hardly more than a cursory glance at the man. Bell said, "This patient is thirty years old. He has just returned from India, where he was a bugler with the Queen's Forty-Sixth Fuseliers. In civilian life, he is now a cobbler. What is more, he is left-handed."

The patient nodded in agreement.

Impressed and incredulous, Bell's students asked how he had arrived at his conclusions.

He answered, "When the man walked into the room, he stood rigidly at attention. His shoes are more brightly polished than those of the average civilian. His face is suntanned, and so he must have just returned from one of our sunny colonies. The *Times* announced the recent return of the regiment I mentioned from India, and the age of repatriation from Her Majesty's colonial forces is thirty. If you observe this patient's chest, it is barrel shaped, expanded by blowing a bugle for many years in service to his country. On the inside of his right knee, outlined on the frayed material of his trousers, are the marks of a shoemaker's last. Since they are on the right side, this man must be left-handed." I would like to think that he also added, "Elementary, my dear students. It is merely a question of observation, deduction, and a reasonable knowledge of the facts."

These three precepts became the guiding principles of Sherlock Holmes's life and work. Although I cannot compare myself to the great detective—and, in fact, I may have embellished the story based on vague childhood recollections of its original version—I would like to think that a psychiatrist follows his avocation in a manner similar to that of Joseph Bell and Sherlock Holmes. The psychiatrist pursues the identification of the offending party—the illness—like a sleuth employing the principles of observation, deduction, and reasonable knowledge of the facts. He constantly remembers the scent being tracked and that the illness rather than the patient is the culprit. The psychiatrist digs and delves into the far reaches of the mind to observe with all the senses the behavior, thinking, and emotions of the patient. The psychiatrist also observes the body and considers its interaction with the mind, and he pays attention to the smallest details in order to unearth the clues that will ultimately lead to the apprehension of the culprit-illness and the rehabilitation of its patient-victim.

·2·

Telltale Symptoms

The language of somatization is not easily understood, because its speakers communicate their emotional discomfort through physical symptoms rather than verbally. The response of families, friends, and physicians may be equally idiosyncratic—their sentiments may range from genuine sympathy to frustration and rage—and may add confusion to already-difficult situations. What results is a Tower of Babel that obscures accurate identification and nomenclature. In recent years, however, psychiatrists have developed an accepted set of terms to define the many different types of somatization. This enables them to diagnose somatization problems more efficiently.

Psychiatrists recognize two types of somatization *symptoms,* functional somatic symptoms and conversion symptoms. Both kinds of symptoms are real, not imagined, and neither kind automatically implies serious emotional problems. Both are reactions to a particular stress at a particular time, each of us responding to stress in our own way. Functional somatic symptoms and conversion symptoms are intermittent, usually passing with the precipitating stress. Each occurs with great frequency in our high-pressure society; and, as I have already noted, few of us can say we have not experienced them at one time or another. They can coexist, and neither is under our voluntary control.

Functional is the term physicians use to designate a condition for which there is no known organic cause. Functional somatic symptoms (FSS) are short-lived somatization symptoms that *directly* express states of emotional discomfort caused by stress. When we are under stress, physical sensations that we would normally ignore can come to signify illness to us; these are FSS. For example, under stress, we may decide a pain in the chest that we usually associate with heartburn and treat with an antacid this time is a heart attack. Or we may think a pain on the right side of the stomach is no longer gas, as usual, but bowel disease.

FSS do not express any hidden (unconscious) meaning. They say, "I am overwhelmed. I find it easier to express my emotional discomfort through physical symptoms than experience emotional discomfort." The symptoms say nothing more than that. They are *not* the mind's way of using illness to avoid a painful situation, elicit sympathy, or gain attention. They can be related to any organ system and can take the forms of headaches, chest pain, palpitations, shortness of breath, tightness in the throat, nausea, retching, abdominal bloating, frequent desire to go to the bathroom, pins and needles, numbness, lower-back pain, and pain anywhere in the body.

Many who experience FSS are often sufficiently insightful to recognize stress as the source of their discomfort, identify the stress, and then take steps to deal with it. This may be as simple as going out for dinner or to a movie; sometimes it may require a more difficult step, such as a change of job or career orientation. When those with FSS do turn to seek medical help, they are more likely to consult their family physicians or medical specialists than psychiatrists. The doctor's reassuring "I cannot find anything wrong" is usually enough to make the FSS go away. But if they suspect stress is involved, doctors may also suggest some form of treatment. They may prescribe mild tranquilizers to relieve emotional discomfort, although tranquilizers do not remove the source of the stress.

Conversion symptoms resemble FSS in their brevity, usually disappearing with the stress that triggered them, but they differ in their psychological structure. Psychiatrically, conversion involves the concept that an emotional conflict is being turned—

converted—into physical symptoms. Conversion symptoms directly express the content of an unconscious conflict that is causing some emotional discomfort. In other words, conversion symptoms have hidden meanings.

Because each person's conflicts are unique, the meaning of each conversion symptom is unique. Because all of us have unconscious conflicts, however, conversion symptoms do not necessarily mean we have significant emotional problems. Rather, the symptoms represent the mind's attempt to resolve the conflict. The symptoms are a way of saying, "It is better to hurt physically than face a conflict full of forbidden ideas that would only make me anxious if I was aware of them. If it looks like I am sick, I'll get lots of sympathy and support." For example, I once treated a heterosexual young man who was having sexual problems. He had a conflict about having sex because his sexual partner represented his mother in his unconscious. Because sex with a parent is taboo, this patient developed a conversion symptom—he lost sensation in his lower abdomen. The symptom allowed him to avoid the frightening situation of having sexual relations with his girlfriend.

Although conversion symptoms allow avoidance of stressful situations and may bring support from family, friends, and physicians (a concept known as primary gain), it is important to remember again that the symptoms are genuinely felt and not sensations consciously willed by the sufferer.

Conversion symptoms contain two other components that set them apart from FSS—the suffering involved represents an element of self-punishment, and the symptoms are generally associated with the nervous system. In fact, conversion symptoms are thought to be the result of a collaboration between the mind and the nervous system, although the exact nature of this relationship is not fully understood.

Pain is the commonest conversion symptom. Others include numbness, pins and needles, muscle twitches, muscle weakness, changes in voice quality, loss of vision, and difficulty swallowing and breathing because the throat feels closed off.

Because FSS and conversion symptoms can both involve neurological symptoms, it is often difficult to distinguish one from the other. Psychiatrists make the distinction only after exploring a patient's thoughts, feelings, and life history to see if there are conflicts behind the symptoms. When a conflict is understood, it always represents a compromise between two unconscious forces—a forbidden wish and the mind's defenses against expressing that wish. The patient whose conversion symptom was a loss of strength in her arm when she got into an argument with her employer was really expressing a wish to hit her boss. Her symptom was not an FSS because I could directly relate it to a special conflict with her employer and not just to the presence of a generally stressful situation at work.

Because the unconscious mind does not always work in such obvious and direct ways, conversion symptoms are more often symbolic, rather than direct, representations of conflicts. A pain in the neck may be a young bride's way of expressing her difficulties with her new mother-in-law. The bride cannot openly say, "You're a pain in the neck," and the pain may help her win support and sympathy, and avoid her mother-in-law.

Similarly, back pain can be a way of saying "Get off my back." This was the case with a seemingly successful, otherwise healthy accountant who developed intermittent, but incapacitating, back pain. Medical evaluations could not account for his condition, and no treatment—ranging from changing his work chair to an exercise program to medication—could provide relief. In desperation, he followed his internist's suggestion and made an appointment to see me. Within a few sessions, it became clear that his back pain was a response to the pressures being put upon him by an overbearing, exacting wife. He invariably felt better and was pain-free when business trips took him to another city. His somatization symptoms were conversion symptoms because they were his way of telling his wife to get off his back.

When hoarseness or a tight, raspy voice are FSS, they are just ways of saying "I am stressed." The nature of the stress is not revealed. But if an analysis of the patient's situation shows that the vocal problems are the patient's way of saying "I am afraid to say what I really think," then the diagnosis is conversion symptoms. The patient's true feelings cannot be expressed openly in words because of unconscious fears and inhibitions. The symptoms speak for the patient, as they do in all forms of somatization.

The intent of any particular conversion symptom is not always obvious when the site of the pain does not directly correspond with the nature of the conflict. For example, a conflict involving unexpressible anger can be converted into shortness of breath—huffing and puffing.

My own experience as an expectant father with neurological symptoms involved, I have since come to realize, conversion symptoms. In my mind, I replaced an emotional conflict—my feelings about my wife's pregnancy and the impending birth of a child—with physical symptoms: twitching leg muscles that I thought meant I had a fatal illness. My symptoms represented an unconscious attempt to deal with a painful conflict activated by my wife's pregnancy. The conflict involved my competitive and negative feelings about the unborn child who threatened to deprive me of my wife's affections. The suffering I experienced was, in part, the punishment I unconsciously imposed on myself for having such negative feelings. The symptoms enabled me to regain my central place in my wife's affections, if only momentarily. They also allowed avoidance of the threatening situation—that is, thinking about the baby. When the neurologist gruffly shooed me from his office, I could not measure the relief I felt. I was so relieved, in fact, that it did not occur to me until much later to ask why a verbally adept individual would express his emotional conflicts as muscle twitches.

If, instead of muscle twitches, I had had paralysis of the legs and my ability to see patients and be a father had been impaired, I would have had a conversion *disorder*. A conversion disorder results in significant physical and emotional dysfunction without physical cause. My twitches did not amount to a physical impairment. Under these circumstances, the individual can avoid stressful activities and get support from family, friends, and physicians that might not otherwise be forthcoming. With conversion symptoms, the avoidance is short-lived and often only indirectly implied and not voluntary; with conversion disorder, avoidance can become a way of life. The attempts to elicit extra care are not implied and ephemeral, as they are in conversion symptoms, but go on for extended periods and are clearly demonstrated. Although the symptoms are initially only unconsciously directed toward these ends and are not under voluntary control, when the sufferers learn that the symptoms are advantageous, they may consciously use their problems to maintain their disabilities and the support systems that accompany them. This is called secondary gain.

Conversion disorders can be mild or extreme and, sometimes, just go away by themselves. A twenty-six-year-old woman's case shows how conversion disorder can become life threatening. After her engagement was broken, she felt her throat was closed off and stopped eating and drinking. Within a few weeks, she had lost thirty-five pounds and was admitted to the hospital with kidney failure due to dehydration. She was barely able to function, but she seemed indifferent to her condition. In the course of our meetings, she said that before they broke up, her boyfriend had been urging her to lose weight and "get down to a size eight from a size twelve." It soon became clear to me that her emotional pain was all being expressed in the physical symptoms associated with the weight loss and dehydration. I showed her how her closed throat, starvation, and illness were an unconscious attempt—albeit unsuccessful—to please her boyfriend, inspire a renewal of their relationship, and show him, with considerable anger, that he was destroying her life. She was now indifferent because all her emotional discomfort had been converted into physical symptoms.

It is patients with conversion disorders such as paralyzed limbs and loss of eyesight or speech who undergo seemingly miraculous, if temporary, cures at revival meetings and religious shrines.

I have performed just such a miracle myself on a twenty-year-old man who had been confined to a wheelchair for five years with paralysis of the legs. When I explained his underlying conflict to him, he stood up—to my and everyone's amazement. He remained standing, although with assistance because of his wasted leg muscles. Within an hour, however, he had returned to his wheelchair, paralyzed once more by his conversion disorder, a condition involving many complicated psychological forces.

Historically, conversion disorder was associated with hysteria, a term of nebulous meaning derived from the Greek word for womb. Over time, the term *hysterical* became associated with a personality style that embraced vanity, self-centeredness, superficiality, and sexual seductiveness with inhibited sexuality and a flair for the dramatic. During the Victorian period, the typical portrait of a patient with hysterical conversion disorder was a young woman who was fragile, flighty, and an invalid with paralysis of her legs, and who had a need for attention and a seeming lack of concern about her symptoms and their implication, called *la belle indifference.* The condition was considered an almost exclusively female malady, and modern researchers have noted that conversion disorders are indeed more prevalent in women.

Research into the different forms and causes of somatization is relatively new, and psychiatrists are far from a full understanding of them. Stress is a major contributor, but it is not the only one and does not appear to act alone. Somatization symptoms are widespread because stress is, but studies show that certain predisposing factors also exist. The most important of these appears to be psychological. It seems that any understanding of somatization must include a knowledge of childhood experiences—indeed, the first moments of life. At that early stage, the world of the infant is the world of the body, and any sense of "self" derives almost exclusively from physical sensations. The infant breathes, smells, tastes, swallows, and eliminates—physical sensations that provide the first confirmation that it exists. Not yet capable of emotional or verbal expression, babies are not happy or sad, and they do not love or hate. If infants could report feelings, they would most likely be states of comfort or discomfort. Hungry or in pain, or well fed, snuggled, and warm, infants judge the world around them on the basis of what is happening to their bodies. The language of somatization resembles these early modes of communication. While natural for an infant, this does not correspond to the normal condition of a mature adult or allow full and effective functioning within society.

We need to identify emotions and express them in words, and to do this, we need to develop separate identities, a process that is at once intricate and sensitive. We also must learn to associate parts of the body with more than anatomical significance. For instance, arms and hands become more than appendages that wave and lift. They offer a means of emotional expression that allow us to touch ourselves and others, and express approval or disapproval.

In theory, those who have successfully navigated the admittedly rough waters of development will be less likely to have somatization symptoms. At times of stress, they are sustained because they can call upon inner reserves of comfort afforded them by a mental image of a comforting mother from whom they have successfully separated. Such people can soften the hard knocks of life and discuss their feelings in terms that family and friends can comprehend and respond to with feeling and advice. The ability to gauge the emotional flavor and nuances of both supportive and stressful responses is an outcome of successful early childhood emotional development.

Most of us do not develop ideally. Our experiences and emotional states vary widely, as do the ways in which we express them physically and verbally. That is why some of us have somatization symptoms more than others. In their milder forms, somatization symptoms may represent no more than a temporary retreat to infantile physical behavior in the presence of stress. At the same time, we do not lose the ability to recognize our emotional discomfort or communicate verbally. The balance between the verbal and physical expressions varies from individual to individual and from situation to situation.

It is not clear why somatization symptoms become either FSS or conversion symptoms. Although both are related to a regression to infantile ways, conversion symptoms may include other developmental factors that influence the expression of conflict, behavior, and memory. Conversion symptoms are frequent in people with medical illness; although there is no clinical proof of it, they may involve a response to the particular stresses and conflicts surrounding medical illness.

We have now seen how modern psychiatry has distinguished between different groups of somatization symptoms, considered the reasons for their existence as part of the mind/body relationship, and determined when conversion symptoms become disorders. It remains to be seen, however, what happens when soma-tization symptoms persist over time and someone becomes preoc-cupied with medical illness and fears of having medical illness, resulting in emotional disabilities. When this happens, we have an emotional disorder called hypochondria.

·3·

Hypochondria

Not long ago, when I was a guest in a fashionable European home, the woman seated on my right at dinner asked what kind of patients I saw. I knew that my hosts and their friends were partial to imbibing those colored tonics, formulated to energize, soothe, and restore, sold in European apothecaries. I also knew that my hostess delighted in displaying and sharing the contents of her Cartier pillbox—tranquilizers, sleeping pills, antibiotics, vitamins. With this in mind, I decided to take a provocative tack.

I said, "Right now, I am engaged in a study of hypochondriacs."

Several of the guests turned toward me. A protracted silence ensued, and I could feel the anxiety level around the table rising.

"You mean those fakers who are always complaining and running to doctors?" a woman across the table asked, breaking the silence. "Why bother with those phonies?"

Another guest asked, "Is that a disease?"

"Oh, I have a friend who is a hypochondriac," our hostess said. "She's forever going to doctors, and they are always putting her in the hospital for exploratory something or other. They never find anything wrong with her. Costs her husband a fortune, flying her around all the time. I guess the insurance picks up the rest. I don't know how he can stay with her."

Of course, a formal dinner party was hardly the venue for a lengthy discourse on hypochondria. But the incident serves as a reminder of just how ill defined and misunderstood the concept of hypochondria is. In today's psychiatric usage, *hypochondriac* refers to a person with the relatively recently defined disorder *hypochondriasis,* and *hypochondria* indicates the symptoms. To avoid confusion, I use the general term *hypochondria* as often as possible when discussing present-day cases.

To the uninitiated, hypochondria may indeed be a nonillness, hardly worth bothering with. Many people, including doctors, question whether it is a genuine syndrome. Is it merely a cluster of attitudes and behaviors no more psychiatric in nature than those of political activists or religious crusaders? Is it an exaggerated interest in body functions similar to that possessed by fashion models and body builders? Is it illness faked in an attempt to gain advantage? The answer is, none of the above.

Hypochondria is an emotional disorder involving unremitting fears of illness and somatization symptoms that last for more than six months and cause significant disability. When it exists on its own, distinct from any other emotional disorder, it is also known as primary hypochondria.

Physical examinations and routine laboratory tests with favorable results do not reassure people with hypochondria. No matter how persuasive the evidence, they insist on interpreting any and every physical change or sensation as conclusive evidence of physical illness. As in the other forms of somatization, their symptoms are genuinely felt and not consciously fabricated.

The symptoms of hypochondria can involve any part of the body, but patients most often cite the head and neck, a region involved in all forms of somatization. These are followed in frequency by the abdomen, chest, sexual organs, and skin. Lower-back pain is also a familiar symptom. Relatively speaking, hypochondria can be mild and result in only occasional absenteeism and an inability to enjoy social or sexual relationships. However, when hypochondria is severe, the ability to work is impaired and relationships with family, friends, and physicians are disrupted. In most cases, hypochondria is not time limited. In fact, it can last a lifetime, with the sufferer, at best, leading a highly restricted and isolated existence and, at worst, becoming an invalid, affirming society's verdict that they are weak and useless.

With our more precise definition of hypochondria has come a more accurate estimate of its incidence (rate of occurrence of new cases), its prevalence (overall number of cases), and its causes. Many researchers say the prevalence of hypochondria is 3 to 13 percent in different cultures. Studies indicate that it begins most often between the ages of twenty and thirty and is spread equally between men and women. Moreover, the condition is notoriously difficult to treat and invariably proves to be costly for the patient, insurers, and the society that ultimately pay its costs.

Like other forms of somatization, the symptoms of hypochondria express emotional discomfort, but their persistence suggests a deeper significance: an attempt to permanently distance and insulate oneself from dealing with emotional discomfort. Through somatization symptoms, the hypochondria patient is saying, "My symptoms are necessary. I need them because they keep the emotional discomfort away. I don't have to face emotional discomfort if I have physical discomfort." In this way, the physical symptoms become a security blanket, providing critical protection from the emotions. Because hypochondriacs understandably insist that their problems are purely physical, they rarely consult psychiatrists. They have to see themselves as physically ill: to accept the emotional roots of their illness would deprive them of the carefully constructed defenses they have erected for self-protection. When they finally do approach psychiatrists, it is because they have exhausted all other options: professional, familial, and societal.

Although stress plays an important role in all somatization symptoms, its roll in hypochondria seems to be different, exacerbating rather than provoking the symptoms. In hypochondria, it is as if the symptoms are always burning at low heat, and stress provides the added fuel that ignites the blaze in all its fury.

The case of a young married woman with mild hypochondria illustrates the nature of the illness and the potent role that stress plays in intensifying hypochondriacal symptoms. In her late thirties, Mrs. Raymond had always found the intimacy of a relationship with a man difficult and, for years, had resisted entering into any extended or permanent relationship. When she did marry, it was a decision based to a large degree on societal pressures. Shortly after her marriage to a prominent attorney, she began to experience acute lower-back pain. Over time, it became so bad that she was not able to leave the house. She consulted many specialists, who all said her X-rays showed, at most, mild degeneration of the lower vertebrae. The damage was no more than to be expected in a woman of her age, and not severe enough to account for the intensity of the pain she was describing. Nonetheless, Mrs. Raymond's specialists, anxious to help her, prescribed a back brace, car and chair seats, physical therapies, and painkillers. None proved effective.

Her husband's wealth enabled her to get around the city during the day in a limousine outfitted with a special backrest. When she lunched with friends, she took yet another backrest into restaurants. But when she was at home with her husband, the pain took over and she lay flat on the floor, claiming that this position provided her only source of relief. Even when the couple entertained, she stayed prone on the carpet, surrounded by her guests. She rose, with help, only to go to the dinner table, and sometimes she did not even do that. Mrs. Raymond was the unquestioned focus of attention and sympathy. She slept in a special hospital bed. Sex was out of the question.

Finally, the couple's desperation led her to opt for surgery, although no disk lesion could be confirmed. Mrs. Raymond's convalescence was protracted, and her condition did not improve significantly. Ultimately, the marriage deteriorated to the point of divorce. Once the major stress of her life—marriage—was over, she could sit on a couch, discarded the hospital bed, joined a busy interior-design firm, and traveled about the city—by bus. However, she continued to be hypochondriacal, though less intensely so. She never stopped complaining about some back pain, and whenever she came under inordinate stress, it worsened.

Although we know that stress plays a role in the genesis of hypochondria, we know very little of the roles played by genetic, environmental, and medical factors. Presumably, they are involved in both the cause and continuation of the condition.

• • •

Causation theories abound. One hypothesis holds that hypochondriacal behavior is learned. The person discovers that having hypochondriacal symptoms is the only way to achieve a modus vivendi with someone else or society. If the significant other or society collaborates, the learned behavior pattern is reinforced and becomes a habitual way of dealing with the world. For instance, a dependent person may find that dependency is acceptable to others when it is accompanied by illness. Were this individual healthy, family and friends might not tolerate the slowness of the persons' progress toward independence. In other cases, inadequacies may be accepted in someone unable to perform well as a worker, parent, or spouse if that person is chronically ill.

Another theory accounts for hypochondria by relying on societal factors. Here it is reasoned that a society, increasingly sophisticated and exposed to the latest medical discoveries and trends through the media and preoccupied with the body, its fitness, shape, and well-being, may be more susceptible to hypochondria than one that is deprived of medical information and a growing fitness industry. In her book *Hypochondria: Woeful Imaginings,* Susan Baur discusses at length the relationship between hypochondria and society. She suggests that a new and subjective value system based on what "feels right" or "feels wrong" has come out of our preoccupation with health and fitness. We measure these feelings by the reactions of others, and this concern for the opinion of others in turn leads to a preoccupation with the self. Indeed, self-centeredness is a familiar personality trait in hypochondriacs. Although some people may retreat to religion, politics, or work at times of major life transitions and emotional upheaval, others may turn inward and place unusual emphasis on their health and well-being. They can then use figures of supposed omniscience, such as doctors, as their source of solace.

There is no evidence that societies with less exposure than ours to health and fitness issues have a lower incidence of hypochondria; on the contrary, hypochondria is a worldwide malady. It can thus be safely said that societal factors probably reinforce tendencies to hypochondria rather than cause it, and we must search for the roots of hypochondria in psychological development and genetics.

The theory of hypochondria as a dynamic of learned and reinforced behavior, does not account for a sufferer's individual personality characteristics; they are genetically and environmentally determined. Whether hypochondria is, in whole or in part, genetic or environmental in origin is difficult to establish. Most likely, both factors are involved. Research shows that the parents of those with hypochondria often have somatization symptoms themselves, emphasize health and the body, and are extraordinarily caring and attentive when their children are ill.

People with hypochondria seem to share certain personality features. They are highly dependent, emotionally needy, easily frustrated, prone to resentment, self-centered, and attention seeking. A key to understanding their personalities—and therefore the disorder—may come from a study of a personality disorder called alexithymia, of which hypochondria is a major component. The word *alexithymia* derives from a Greek term meaning "no words for emotions," and someone with an alexithymic personality cannot sense, identify, and express any emotions. Whereas most of us can understand why we feel happy, sad, angry, or calm and express these emotions verbally, alexythymics are unable to do this and have been called "emotional illiterates." Alexithymics are believed not to have developed emotionally beyond the early infantile phase when all communication is physical and babies cannot yet identify their emotions, much less express them.

This progression from physical to emotional expression depends on the infant's ability to differentiate from the mother and form a separate identity. In alexithymics, this process is somehow impaired—by a mother who herself has difficulty expressing emotion or who has difficulty allowing her child to individuate. Instead of venturing out to explore emotionality, the alexithymic remains anchored in the physical realm of infancy. Similarly, hypochondriacs do not seem to have made a smooth or complete transition to a more mature stage where emotions are recognized and verbally described. Instead, they chronically rely on physical symptoms that protect them from emotional discomfort. This stands in sharp contrast to those with intermittent somatization symptoms—that is, FSS—who only retreat to infantile forms of physical expression at times of stress.

If such developmental impairment is common to all hypochondria, then learned behavior, identification with parents who somatize, and cultural influences can be seen as reinforcing, rather than originating, a tendency toward hypochondria. Thus, both developmental and environmental factors become necessary in order for the illness to reach fruition.

Whatever the causes, hypochondriacs do not accept the emotional roots of their illness. Because their physical illnesses keep their emotional distress at bay, they need to see themselves as physically ill and can rarely be persuaded to consult psychiatrists. Rather, people with hypochondria push all other medical professionals to their absolute limits. They leave a trail of bulging charts as they trudge from physician to physician in pursuit of treatment. Certain as they are of their symptoms, they swamp physicians and staff members with their medical histories, believing that they are aiding the diagnostic process with their detailed and precise presentation. They also want to leave no doubt as to the medical origins of their problems.

Hypochondriacs very effectively play on their doctors' kernel of doubt that they may be "missing something." They very cannily sense a doctor's reluctance to assign emotional origins to their physical symptoms, even when blood tests, CAT scans, MRIs, and the like have turned up nothing. Physicians want to arrive at a plausible, accurate diagnosis. Trained to deal with disease, they consider physical illness more serious than psychological illness and take their patients' complaints seriously and at face value. Many simply may not have the time, talent, or knowledge required to detect the subtle psychological clues that hypochondriacs tend to drop.

In their joint endeavor, patients and their doctors strive for some "truth," that is, a medical diagnosis. When doctors cannot arrive at that "truth," they react in different ways. Some pursue diagnoses relentlessly, poring over medical journals in hopes of discovering a rare condition or a symptom or sign that will empower them to draw their conclusions. They turn to vague, unclassified diagnoses like chronic fatigue syndrome, hypoglycemia, multiple allergies, and hidden nutritional deficiencies. They often append the terms *idiopathic* (unknown) and *syndrome* (group of symptoms) to descriptive diagnoses, leading to entries on charts such as "idiopathic fainting syndrome." They refer the patients to specialists in hopes of confirming diagnoses or providing others. They insist that the conditions are not "in the patients' heads" and do not recommend a psychiatric consultation.

Conversely, some physicians may sense early on that these patients have no physical disease and lose interest. They refer the patients elsewhere or bluntly inform them that there is nothing physically wrong with them and that they should "get their act together." Some doctors wash their hands of the problem by prescribing mild tranquilizers that relieve patients' emotional discomforts—and their own. Sometimes they prescribe medications just for their placebo effects.

Patients with hypochondria may become frustrated, angry, and argumentative. They claim they are not getting the proper care. Physicians tire of seeing these patients and refer them elsewhere.

Some patients with hypochondria demand that their doctors be brilliant and even godlike. When one physician fails them, they switch to another, encouraging each new practitioner with a litany of the failures of those who came before. Proud of their reputations as diagnosticians and not ones to shy away from challenges, these new doctors take up the patients' causes, yearning to discover the undiscovered. The cycle of diagnostic investigations begins again.

Some hypochondriacs seek personal and emotional relationships with their doctors. They use physicians as unwitting sources for psychotherapy, gaining some comfort from the relationship without having to control the emotional origins of their distress. They make inordinate demands on the physicians' time, in the office and on the telephone, presenting every phone call as an emergency, and ultimately causing feelings of frustration and impotence on the part of their doctors. If they do find sympathetic physicians, their beliefs that their problems are purely physical are reinforced and they may even increase their symptoms if they find their doctors responding with greater interest and more intensive care. By denying or dismissing the possibility that their patients' syndromes may have emotional origins, doctors can denigrate the value of psychiatric treatment and stand in the way of appropriate care.

In most instances, patients with hypochondria do not find the level of sensitivity they seek, and the doctor-patient relationship deteriorates. A catch-22 situation can result. If a doctor stops treating a patient, the patient may distort the doctor's reasons and interpret the disrupted relationship as additional proof that doctors don't know what they are doing. If a doctor decides that a patient's symptoms have emotional origins, that doctor may neglect to adequately scrutinize that patient's next set of complaints and possibly miss genuine physical illness. Moreover, if the diagnostic tests that a doctor orders are invasive, they may carry the risk of complications. The same holds true for medications, many of which have unpleasant side effects.

When hypochondria alone is the disorder responsible for the symptoms, it is known as primary hypochondria. Diagnosis of hypochondria, however, is made difficult by the fact that it does not always exist as a separate emotional disorder. As mentioned before, when hypochondria is part of another, treatable emotional disorder, it is called secondary hypochondria. Secondary hypochondria can accompany a depressive disorder, generalized anxiety disorder, panic disorder, obsessive compulsive disorder, or some psychotic disorders, such as monosymptomatic hypochondriacal psychosis, delusional depressive disorder, delusional disorder, and schizophrenia. Because of its association with these disorders, secondary hypochondria is the form of hypochondria psychiatrists see most frequently. When the emotional disorder that causes them is treated, the symptoms of secondary hypochondria can be reduced in intensity or reversed altogether. Therefore, all people with persistent somatization symptoms deserve a psychiatric consultation.

Secondary hypochondria can be difficult to understand until you see how it actually interacts with another emotional disorder. When we speak about disorders, we need to recall that a person has a disorder when the symptoms are sufficiently severe to interfere significantly with everyday living. Having depressed feelings does not amount to having a depressive disorder; having anxious feelings is not equivalent to an anxiety disorder; nor do feelings of panic indicate a panic disorder.

Secondary hypochondria is a frequent companion of depressive disorder (also sometimes called major or clinical depression), a biologically rooted condition that presents itself with a mixture of emotional and physical symptoms. Nearly all patients with depressive disorder are thoroughly evaluated by at least an internist and usually other specialists before the psychiatrist sees them. The case of Helen Lewis shows some of the hallmark symptoms of depressive disorder.

Mrs. Lewis had seen an internist, gynecologist, and nephrologist before she was referred to me. In her seventies, she complained of pain. Although she seemed to have no trouble specifying the location of her pain—in the vagina—to other medical specialists, perhaps her age and my specialty made her reluctant to name its location. Her modesty gave me the clue to just where the pain was. I could have remained frustrated if I had insisted on hearing it from her. Instead, I helped the process along.

"Is it down below?" I asked.

"Yes," she answered, almost managing a smile, "it's terrible. It's there day and night. I can't sleep. It keeps me up all night. I have so much pain, I don't think to eat anymore. It makes me so tired. I am so tired, I don't want to do anything. I just stay in the house. No wonder I'm so tired, I'm not eating, I'm not sleeping. The pain exhausts me."

Like so many people with depressive disorder, she did not say she felt depressed. She said she was upset because of her physical symptoms. She looked depressed. Her dress was soiled, her hair was unwashed and uncombed, and she smelled as if she had not been bathing. Clearly she had not been taking care of herself.

"There's nothing that can be done for me," she said, confirming the depressive's typical sense of hopelessness. "This pain is never going to go away."

These vaginal sensations overwhelmed this elderly woman with guilt. Her husband had passed away some years before and now the vaginal pain, which she associated with sexual feelings, was akin to adultery. The persistent pain she felt "down below" was a symptom of secondary hypochondria. After a course of antidepressant medication, her depression was treated and the pain went away.

Both the ambiguity and the precise knowledge that we have of hypochondria reflect modern medicine's emphasis on disease rather than illness and hypochondria's colorful history. In Western societies, practicing and research physicians study pathology—that is, disease—with greater interest than the patients' perceptions and responses to pathology—that is, illness. Conversely, in many Eastern cultures, doctors and societies emphasize the universal nature of all illness, whether or not physical pathology is present. No shame is associated with hypochondria—and other forms of somatization—and Eastern physicians apply the same principles of treatment to illness, whether physical or emotional in origin.

Over the millennia, hypochondria has been in and out of fashion and the public consciousness. It has attracted the attention of physicians, philosophers, and conjurers. The term itself originates with Hippocrates, who related it to a connection between fevers and disease under the rib cage. Hence *hypo,* meaning under, and *chondros,* the cartilage of the ribs or the organs of the upper abdomen: liver, gallbladder, spleen, stomach, and duodenum. In the second century A.D., Galen paved the way for its modern connotations when he linked it to a broad range of digestive disorders without apparent physical cause.

Biographies of famous people who have suffered from the malady provide us with wonderful examples of how hypochondria can originate and affect its victims and those who treat and interact with them. Such biographies also demonstrate how perceptions about the illness have resisted change, despite more precise psychiatric definition. The examples I have chosen—Marcel Proust, the French novelist, and Charles Darwin, the British naturalist—are but two in a long line of famous sufferers of hypochondria.

Proust suffered from hypochondriacal symptoms as well as asthma, a psychosomatic illness. We now understand that acute asthma attacks are often precipitated by emotional stress, and throughout Proust's life there are indications that his asthma worsened whenever he felt unloved by his mother. One remembered childhood episode followed when his mother withheld an eagerly anticipated good-night kiss as a form of punishment. Moreover, his mother seemed to thrive on his being ill and took responsibility for his treatment, saying "The doctor may be cleverer than I am, but I know what is right."

Proust's mother also appears to have withdrawn her affection during her son's periods of health, a behavior Proust was aware of. He wrote, "The truth is . . . that the moment I'm well, as the way of life which makes me well infuriates you, you demolish everything until I am ill again. . . . It's very sad not to be able to have affection and health both at once." Proust's experience, as we now know, was not an uncommon one. A history of increased parental love and attention during illness figures prominently in the histories of hypochondriacs.

Proust thus remained "sickly," and illness became a constant companion, ultimately one of the few in his increasingly isolated life. Whereas much of this can be attributed to an unconscious need to retain his mother's affections, he also used his preoccupation with illness to avoid social or professional engagements. If the prospect of seeing a friend or a speaking engagement was too potentially stressful, he developed physical symptoms and invoked illness as an excuse to cancel the meetings. This behavioral pattern shows how Proust avoided stressful situations with somatization symptoms, an indication of how hypochondria enables the person to insulate himself from the vicissitudes of life.

Proust's father was a physician, and his role as a provider of medical care may also have contributed to his son's hypochondriasis. In any case, Proust's relationships with physicians were also typical of the hypochondriac's. As one of his biographers wrote, "Psychiatrists are familiar with the patient who sets impossible conditions for his treatment, abandons it if he sees any risk of being cured, knows enough about the secret causes of his neurosis to be able to parry all attempts to detect them, and begins by establishing a feeling of intellectual superiority over his doctor. So it was to be with . . . Proust, who unconsciously preferred his asthma, and the way of life it necessitated, to the health of ordinary human beings."

By jealousy guarding his symptoms and ultimately disparaging the medical profession that could not confirm the source of illness, Proust showed the personality type of many chronic somatizers. He always anticipated the worst: for at least fifteen years, he announced his imminent death. His friends were amused. One remembered saying to him, "You seem the picture of health." Proust replied, "Dear friend, I have nearly died three times since morning."

True to type, Proust had a detailed knowledge of things medical and, like his mother, imagined himself to have more knowledge than his physicians. He resorted to self-medication and often took one medicine to counter the effects of another. Consequently, and not unexpectedly, he experienced genuine symptoms that prompted ever greater preoccupations with his health. When caffeine failed him as a stimulant, he turned to Adrenalin. Both were to offset the "narcotic aftereffects" of Veronal, a sleeping medication. One one occasion, to ready himself for an evening with friends, he took an undiluted amount of Adrenalin. His throat and stomach burned for hours afterward, and for a month he lived on ice cream and cold beer. Like other people with hypochondria, Proust worried about illness for which there was no physical evidence. He once tried to convince the famous physician Babinski to "open his skull" for an imagined brain tumor.

People with hypochondria are extremely close observers of their bodily activities and changes, however subtle. These detailed observations allow them to confer elaborate meanings on physical changes and attribute them to the physical illness of which they invariably have detailed knowledge. This attention to minute detail came through in Proust's literary style, and it is interesting to note that he was at his most productive during periods of acute hypochondriacal episodes.

Hypochondriacs are equally as responsive to environmental modifications. Proust feared drafts. He worried about the effects of noise and, at one point, secluded himself in a cork-lined room at the Ritz in Paris.

Assuming symptoms that mimic those of a loved one can be the hypochondriac's way of holding on to a deceased individual for months or even a lifetime. Proust so identified with his mother that he took on her symptoms when she was ill and dying. As he approached his own death, the causes of Proust's symptoms became increasingly "mysterious" and "complex." He did not think that his brain was affected, although his physicians held his abuse of narcotics and stimulants accountable for his obviously altered state. At one point, Proust diagnosed himself as having chronic uremia, a condition that could have certainly been caused by his use of drugs, as could his lack of coordination. Most interestingly, these symptoms, as Proust himself observed, replicated those of his mother in her final illness.

As Proust approached his death, he did so with surprising calm, given the terror he had previously shown. He had contracted influenza, and it lingered on for weeks. Feverish, coughing, and short of breath, he rejected the idea of going to a nearby clinic and remained instead in his unheated room. He adopted a regimen of fasting and made it clear to all who visited that he could not recover and did not want to. With the powers afforded by hindsight, I cannot help but wonder whether Proust's sense of helplessness and his refusal of food were not signs of a depressive disorder.

Just as the life of Marcel Proust reveals some telling details about the origins of hypochondria, its facilitation by family, its requirement of frequent medical attention, its serious consequences, and, possibly its influence in the production of literary masterpieces, that of Charles Darwin reveals some telling details about hypochondria and the prejudices that accompany its identification. For years, beginning well before his historic voyage on the *Beagle* in 1831, Darwin complained of palpitations, pains around the heart, retching, headaches, stomach pains, fatigue, and general indisposition. He believed that the genesis of his maladies was physical, as can be seen from these entries in his personal journal, dated 1848.

> From July to the end of the year, unusually unwell with swimming of head, depression, trembling, many bad attacks of sickness.

> Very little fatigue, or excitement or anxiety (of which I should have plenty) almost invariably brings on so much swimming of the head, nausea and other symptoms, the effect of sitting 2 or 3 (or even less) [hours] in a public chair would be quite intolerable to me.

Unquestionably productive and prolific, Darwin was nonetheless aware that his symptoms inhibited his productivity, as he reported in his diary: ". . . did very little on account of being unwell . . ." and ". . . wasted some time by being unwell."

Both Darwin's contemporaries and modern biographers have debated whether he was a hypochondriac, and if so, to what extent. During his lifetime, his doctors' opinions swung from diagnoses of hypochondria to organic illness. Darwin's own assessment of his health paralleled his physicians'.

In the century since his death, physicians have speculated that he had contracted and carried the rare illness Chagas' disease, which might have resulted from an insect bite while he was in Argentina. Other medical experts dispute this, saying Chagas' disease was unlikely because in the final decade of Darwin's life, his health was better than it had been for the preceding thirty years. They also note that the symptoms Darwin described were present before he could have been bitten by the disease-carrying insect. Differences of opinion among doctors are frequent when it comes to hypochondria.

One Darwin biographer, R. W. Clark, doubted Darwin's hypochondria, although he acknowledged that the naturalist "may occasionally have overstressed ill health as a reason for avoiding social duties he disliked," an idea echoed by Sir Peter Medawar, the English biologist and Nobel laureate. Medawar wrote, "Ill people suspected of hypochondria or malingering have to pretend to be iller than they really are and may then get taken in by their own deception. They do this to convince others." Sir Arthur Keith, the late-nineteenth-century anatomist and anthropologist, dismissed the idea of hypochondria, claiming that Darwin's ailments were felt, not imagined. This view suggests that then, as now, hypochondria was seen as malingering—the feigning of illness for conscious gain. It also reveals the widely held belief, unfounded, that hypochondriacs do not really experience their symptoms. Ultimately, Clark did state: "Darwin's illness may have been, at least in part, the result of a mental conflict created by his work."

John Bowlby, the English psychiatrist and psychoanalyst, tries to explain Darwin's symptoms in his 1991 book, *Charles Darwin: A New Life*. Bowlby finds overwhelming evidence for somatization as the cause of the naturalist's physical symptoms. Bowlby assigns four causes to Darwin's somatization: a predisposing constitution and provoking, contributing, and symptom-specifying factors.

A predisposing constitution refers to an inherent susceptibility to an illness. Provoking causes refer to stresses that, in Darwin's case, at least, Bowlby believes might have been pressures to produce and stresses emanating from his family life. Here Bowlby speaks of his wife's pregnancies, the frequent illnesses of his children, and his father's death. However, as Bowlby mentions, stressful events are a universal cause of anxiety, but they do not necessarily lead to emotional breakdown or to somatization.

Bowlby suggests that Darwin's vulnerability to these stresses and his subsequent somatization arose from difficult family relationships during his childhood and adolescence. These are contributing causes. Bowlby attempts to link Darwin's symptoms to the death of his mother when Darwin was a young boy, the family silence surrounding her death, and the family's reluctance ever to mention Mrs. Darwin's death in the ensuring years. Because of this silence, Bowlby feels that Darwin may have assumed a sense of responsibility for his mother's death. He also cites Charles Darwin's "difficult, though far from bad relations with his father."

Symptom-specifying causes refer to events that promote particular expressions of an illness in the individual. In Darwin's case, this refers to the site and nature of his symptoms—stomach, heart, skin. Bowlby associates this with Darwin's inability to withstand painful thoughts and the consequent expression of these unwanted emotional states as physical symptoms. Bowlby does not provide a specific understanding of how emotional factors and the site of somatization are linked.

Bowlby feels that had Darwin lived in our era, he would have benefited from psychotherapy and physiotherapy. The psychotherapy would have given him insight into his tendency to hyperventilate when he was anxious, into the nature and origins of his anxieties, and into his dismissal of painful thoughts. The physiotherapy would have taught him how to breathe properly. Bowlby also proposes that Darwin had panic disorder, now known to be a cause of secondary hypochondria.

Today, I think Darwin would be diagnosed as having primary and secondary hypochondria. Undoubtedly, Darwin would have benefited from psychotherapy that would have helped him understand that his physical symptoms were related to his emotional state. In addition, one feels his life would have been quite different if one of his physicians had been able to prescribe one of the many medications we now have that ameliorate depressive disorders.

Reviewing the lives of Darwin and Proust, one cannot help but be impressed that their hypochondria did not inhibit their genius or impair their productivity. Not every sufferer has been so fortunate. Even in our own time, when the illness is better understood and psychiatric treatment is available, many hypochondriacs go untreated or resist treatment. When they are helped, they are like the unjustly imprisoned coming into light and freedom after time in the darkness.

The intricacies and complexities of somatization rarely reveal themselves in an open-and-shut manner; rather, they unfold slowly, often over years. The psychiatrist is faced with the task of pursuing all the clues that will reveal the types of somatization and guide the treatment. Sometimes repeatedly, psychiatrists may miss these signs, even the obvious ones. They may unwittingly follow road signs purposely turned in the wrong direction, and if they lose the spoor, they may or may not stumble back on the right track. A case may never be fully resolved. As you read the case histories, you may know where the clues are leading before I did at the time. By way of explanation, I ask you to understand that clues are often more difficult to sort out in the emotion-laden atmosphere of the treatment situation.

As you will observe from the case histories, the treatment of psychiatric patients, with or without somatization problems, is difficult. Any "they-lived-happily-ever-after" outcomes of psychiatric treatment are essentially quasi-fiction and, in their resolution, imitate theater rather than reality. If successful, psychiatric treatment can provide a new beginning to life's adventures, not an end in itself. We can only guess what will happen in the future to anyone who has finished or left treatment. Therefore, I have left many of the case histories open-ended and refrained from predicting the patients' futures or from gracing the stories with universal significance. I feel that every reader will have her or his own interpretations and will not need to be encumbered by mine.

Thus, the histories that follow are not just the stories of the hypochondriacs I have encountered in my years of practice. They are stories of the challenges and difficulties I have faced treating them and, on occasion, the rewards they, their families, and I have reaped when that treatment has been successful—in one instance, in ways I could not have anticipated.

PART TWO

. . .

Six People

·4·

The Suffering
Septuagenerian

Until I met Richard Reynolds, a septuagenarian who suffered from lifelong hypochondriasis, I had had little experience with hypochondria in older people. But Mr. Reynolds altered my lifetime perceptions of how illness manifests itself in the older person: I realized that age adds a diabolical dimension to the symptoms and care of hypochondria.

From childhood on, Mr. Reynolds's life had been suffused with symptoms. His was a life dominated by illness, real and imagined. Under his inadvertent tutelage, I learned that two factors color the clinical picture of primary hypochondriasis in the elderly. The first is the very real increased likelihood of physical illness; the second is retirement, which for many, is highly stressful, and also allows for more time to dwell on the state of one's health. Physically vulnerable, and more acutely aware of their every physical sensation, elderly patients find validity in their concerns and are increasingly preoccupied with them. It is also hard to distinguish the physical from the emotional in the elderly, which makes them more difficult to treat. Consequently, mistakes are made and the choice of treatment is often inappropriate.

Doctors who know that a patient is hypochondriacal make allowances for this fact, but doctors seeing a patient with hypochondria for the first time without the benefit of an extensive history may emphasize the physical and neglect the psychological. To complicate the picture, as we have said, hypochondriacs consult many doctors and may vary the presentation of their history from office to office, depending on the physicians' styles and questions asked. The same holds true for much of the rest of the senior population.

Richard Reynolds was a patient on the medical ward, for severe abdominal and back pain, when I was initially called in as a consultant on his case. I was called in as much for the benefit of the ward nurses as for his, because they were unable to control his behavior. Mr. Reynolds screamed—not moaned, as patients in pain are apt to do. He disturbed everyone on the ward by day and kept them awake by night. His behavior was unacceptable by hospital standards.

On my way to the ward, I thought about the reasons psychiatrists are called to consult on medical wards. In my experience, I was seen as the physician who could help a medically ill patient deal with the varied, sometimes exaggerated, but not unexceptional behaviors that illness can trigger. Although being upset, anxious, and blue are normal responses to illness, patient behavior on occasion exceeds these norms. These patients reject their doctor's recommendations, resist treatment, disobey orders, and make inordinate demands on the staff. Intervening in such situations is certainly a necessary role for the psychiatrist to play. But psychiatrists also have to accomplish another, perhaps more important, task. They must make a diagnosis. Psychiatrists have to determine if the patient's symptoms are a direct emotional response to medical illness, if they are a direct effect of the illness, or if the medical illness is a manifestation of a psychiatric condition. To complicate matters, these conditions can coexist in a number of configurations.

Before meeting Mr. Reynolds, I spoke with the nursing staff. They were at their wits' end. They said the patient was like a baby, with no sense of time, screaming around the clock, and intensifying his outcries at night when he was unable to sleep. His cries of "Help me, help me, help me, help me" and "I'm in pain, I'm in pain, I'm in pain, I'm in pain" had set them all on edge. The staff construed his behavior as willful. In their opinion, he screamed because he wanted attention, a common perception of disturbed behavior by those who must live with or care for the emotionally distraught. Neither television nor radio could silence, distract, or keep him in a bed or chair. He stalked the halls and haunted the nurses' station, intrusive and disruptive.

I was a court of last resort. His physicians had prescribed potent painkillers and tranquilizers in ever-increasing doses and got inversely proportionate results. They were perplexed; the staff was desperate. "Help us, help us," a staff member parodied the patient. This is not to say that the staff had not tried different strategies to help Mr. Reynolds. They answered his cries; they ignored them; they tried to soothe him; finally, they yelled at him. Now, when all else had failed, they summoned a psychiatrist.

I listened to the nursing staff and then studied the patient's chart. I had to know what his other physicians had thought. I had to assess his metabolic status through his blood chemistry tests. Knowing which drugs had been prescribed was critical. All the while, I was unable to ignore the piercing screams emanating from the hallway. They were unnerving, more appropriate to a horror movie than a late-twentieth-century hospital setting. Yet I was moved, as if this were an infant crying. My instinctive reaction was to cradle and calm, lessen the suffering and distress. Of course, I could not do this. I suspected that his aberrant behavior was a symptom of his medical condition rather than just an emotional response to his illness.

When I reached Mr. Reynolds, he appeared to know who I was and started to speak immediately, making any formal introduction impossible. "Doctor, I'm in pain. I've been in pain for months. And no one can find the reason for my pain."

As he spoke, I observed. He appeared drugged, barely able to keep his eyes open. He wore a hospital gown, open and untied at the back, which kept slipping off his shoulders, leaving him exposed. His hair was dirty and disheveled, while his nails and buttocks bore unmistakable traces of feces. I was overwhelmed by his shabbiness and loss of dignity.

I find it easier to approach medically ill patients with medical questions rather than with what may be perceived as psychiatric ones. I prefer not to risk alienating a patient who believes his problem to be purely physical.

"Can you tell me something about the pain?" I asked.

"I'm in pain, Doctor. I'm in pain." Mr. Reynolds could say nothing else, no matter how much I urged him. His response was almost a chant: "I'm in pain, Doctor. I'm in pain."

People who perseverate (blurt out words or phrases repeatedly) often are not in full command of their mental faculties. I wondered whether this patient fell into that category.

My medical questions were getting me nowhere, so I switched to psychiatric questioning techniques and began a formal testing of his intellectual status.

"Have we met before, Mr. Reynolds?" This question is designed to test the patient's memory. Sometimes, to cover up a loss of memory, the patient lies and may even offer details of imaginary past meetings.

"Yes, I remember," he answered, but could not go on. "I'm in pain."

I became more direct. "What is the date today, Mr. Reynolds?"

"I never read the newspaper."

This is a common response from patients who do not know the date. I asked the question again, and it was clear that he did not know the date.

"Where are you now?"

"I don't know."

"What kind of place is this?"

"I'm in pain. I'm in pain, Doctor."

"Is this a hotel, a store, a hospital?"

"A hotel."

"Can you tell me how many nickels make a dollar twenty-five cents?"

"I'm in pain. I'm in pain."

I did not have the heart to continue, nor did I need to. With just a few questions, my suspicions were aroused. Was Richard Reynolds delirious? Perserveration, disorientation, and confabulations are definitive signs of delirium. Delirium can be caused by any number of illnesses originating in either the body or the brain. Infections, altered metabolic states, and medications are common bodily causes of delirium, particularly in the elderly.

The signs of delirium can range from a mild and barely noticeable diminution in consciousness to severe psychosis. Awareness and concentration are diminished, and the patient is disoriented. Memory is impaired, and simple intellectual functions like calculating basic money problems become challenging. As the severity of the delirium increases, so does the inability to recognize people or objects. Agitation is the most troubling symptom. Delirious patients are unable to remain still, continuously plucking on the bed sheets or clothing, refusing to stay in bed, and feverishly pacing when they don't. Delirious patients are likely to become delusional or to hallucinate. They can injure themselves. Disoriented and unable to comprehend the attachment of an encumbering apparatus to their body, they often tear out IV tubes.

Disoriented but not delusional, Mr. Reynolds was only moderately delirious. His situation was analogous to waking up in a hotel room for the first time and for a few seconds not realizing where you are. Mr. Reynolds had this sense of disorientation all the time.

My recognition of his delirium was not sufficient. I had to locate its causes. Some could be ruled out immediately. His hospital record indicated that the CAT scan of his brain was normal. His blood chemistries also were all normal, ruling out an obviously altered metabolism. Detective-style, I turned my attention to the list of his medications. It included two major tranquilizers and three potent painkillers. By a process of exclusion, I concluded that these drugs had caused and perpetuated his delirium rather than relieving his symptoms, and I recommended that these medicines be stopped. Over the next few days, Mr. Reynolds's cries of pain diminished "miraculously," as a member of the nursing staff put it.

Twenty-four hours later, when I returned to check on his progress, Mr. Reynolds smiled, if only weakly, and began a conversation. He spoke in short, clipped sentences, spitting out his words, but he no longer perseverated and now could tell me why he had been hospitalized. He seemed to welcome me as the newest superstar on his medical team, giving me the impression that he expected I would be the one to truly help him.

"I've had months of symptoms, Doctor. Severe lower abdominal pain. Down here." He ran his hand across his lower abdomen. "I've lost weight. Fifteen pounds. I can't eat. I can't sleep.

My doctors don't know nothing. They've looked up and down. Every test. They don't know nothing. You—you really seem to know what you're doing. Doctor, please help me."

Our brief conversation and his final plea for my help, combined with what I had learned about Reynolds from his physicians and the hospital record, gave me pause. I contemplated diagnoses. Depressive disorder? Depressive disorder can be a cause of pain, often severe, for which no physical cause can be found. In Reynolds's case, the clues fit nicely into place: his loss of appetite and insomnia were typical symptoms of this disorder. And despite countless blood tests, bowel X-rays, a colonoscopy, and even an abdominal CAT scan, the cause of his pain remained elusive.

As it turned out, Mr. Reynolds's preoccupation with his pain made it impossible for him to give a full history. In addition, his physicians' failure to pick up or record any evidence of hypochondria, and his presenting symptoms of depressive disorder, detoured me at the time from pursuing a more complete history and weighing a diagnosis of hypochondria. In retrospect, I suspect the praise of my colleagues and the gratitude of the nursing staff may have made me overly self-confident. I was now eager to pursue what I thought was "the truth" about Richard Reynolds.

No longer screaming but still complaining of abdominal pain, Mr. Reynolds remained hospitalized. I waited a week, however, before introducing any new medication. I wanted to make sure the tranquilizers and painkillers had been excreted from his system before proceeding. Continuing to believe in my diagnosis of depressive disorder, I prescribed an antidepressant in hopes that it would reverse the symptoms of depressive disorder and abolish his pain.

What I failed to take into account was that, in less than thirty-six hours after our first meeting and the withdrawal of his medications, his pain began subsiding on its own, without my help and for no apparent reason. He was soon discharged, but not before he made an appointment to see me privately.

A week after his release, Mr. Reynolds arrived at my office accompanied by his wife. He was no longer the pathetic, unkempt, disheveled patient I had encountered in the hospital. He was a good-looking, indeed handsome, man, impeccably tailored and meticulously groomed. He was boyish, despite his years.

I had only seen Mrs. Reynolds intermittently in the hospital. Short and plump, neatly but simply dressed, she sat across from him. She's a brooding hen, I thought. In fact, I was reminded of a scene from a documentary of the life of the pianist Vladimir Horowitz in which the young virtuoso, perfectly dressed, his hair slicked down, was sitting next to his proud and beaming mother.

From the outset, Mrs. Reynolds established a pattern that would repeat itself at most of our meetings: she did the talking. He was given little opportunity to speak.

"Doctor, he has not been this well in years. It's miraculous. You have helped him so much; we are grateful. I hope he stays well. He's had such a hard time. Illness after illness."

"Tell me about his illness from the beginning," I said, not realizing I had taken to addressing the patient's wife rather than the patient.

"He had a nervous breakdown in his twenties. He heard that one of his friends died. He was depressed again—I don't recall when. He was also depressed when his father died—about eighteen years ago."

Here was a confirmation of my diagnosis. Depressive disorder is recurrent.

Mrs. Reynolds continued, "He retired ten years ago when he had his heart attack. He keeps insisting he feels lonely and needs me at home with him. If I stopped working, I don't know what would happen to me. It's the only chance I get to have a rest. As it is, he calls me at work several times a day. He calls the ambulance to take him to the emergency room, then calls me to meet him there. Some days, he goes out with his friends. He's happier then, when he's watching the prices at the stockbroker's. But mainly he complains of being sick all the time. I'm scared the doctors are going to miss something. I know for years they've all said there's nothing wrong with him, that it's all in his mind. But what if something is wrong? He's not so young anymore. He's at an age when people start to get serious problems. I feel the doctors are overlooking this. He's already had two heart attacks and has a pacemaker. He has arthritis. He's had to go to the hospital so many times. Sometimes they just see him in the emergency room; sometimes they have to admit him."

With the session about to end, I had one question that I felt had to be posed at that first office meeting. I wanted to know why Mrs. Reynolds had not gotten a companion to stay with her husband.

"Wouldn't this ease your burden?" I asked.

"I can't afford it," she said. "I spend enormous amounts of money on my husband's medical care, even with the insurance reimbursements." Mrs. Reynolds repeated this answer whenever I broached the issue of finding help.

It was during this first visit with the Reynoldses as a couple that I began to experience doubts as to the accuracy of my diagnosis of depressive disorder. I did not act on these suspicions, however. Because Mr. Reynolds seemed to be doing well, I scheduled an appointment in a month's time and renewed his prescription for the antidepressant medication that I thought had conquered his pain.

Four weeks later, the Reynoldses returned to my office for their second appointment. He was again a changed man. Gone was the neatly pressed designer suit and carefully combed hair. He looked haggard and disheveled, although not to the same degree as when I had encountered him on the medical ward.

"I'm in pain, Doctor," he said, his speech slightly slurred.

"But you were doing so well," I said, trying to reassure myself.

"I'm in pain, Doctor."

Mrs. Reynolds broke in, "The pains seem to come on every day at precisely three in the afternoon—when he gets home from watching the ticker tape. He calls me at work and asks me to come home. I can't, of course. I'm the office manager of an important law firm, and I have responsibilities there. I've tried to explain this to him. He won't listen. I have to give him more and more pain medicine. He also needs tranquilizers—small doses don't help."

Since our last visit, the Reynoldses had made the rounds of his specialists and been to the hospital emergency room at least four times. His list of medicines had lengthened, including new painkillers and tranquilizers. No one had called me. I thought that perhaps Mr. Reynolds had withheld my name.

This time Mr. Reynolds did add to the conversation, mostly to comment that I was listening to Mrs. Reynolds too much.

"I'm in pain. Please help me," he said.

I took a long look at him. He didn't appear as though he was in pain, but I did not doubt his sincerity. Hypochondriacs do not feign their symptoms. And yet, I was beginning to notice that his complaints increased when attention was focused elsewhere, when the nurses were occupied with other patients, his wife with her work, and I with mine—in this instance, getting information from Mrs. Reynolds. When he complained of pain, he bent over, clutched his abdomen, and yelped.

I thought about Mrs. Reynolds and the difficulty of her position. If she didn't get away from him for at least part of the day, the continual demand for care and attention, the constant complaining, and the hovering specter of illness would have overwhelmed her, physically and emotionally. Being at the office provided a necessary respite, but it also put her in a terrible bind. She carried a burden of worry and fear that he would become seriously ill in her absence. She had difficulty distinguishing in the course of a telephone call with him what was "real" and what was psychologically induced.

Mrs. Reynolds expressed her other underlying fears when she said, "Real illness is much more common after seventy." She certainly could keep both of them calmer by making sure he took tranquilizers and painkillers. On the other hand, her strategy had its weaknesses. Her actions reinforced his beliefs that his pain emanated from physical sources, and occasionally those increased dosages made him delirious. At the same time, when he did become delirious, he could be admitted to the hospital and she would be provided with a break. An unending cycle had been set in motion, a cycle to which both Mr. and Mrs. Reynolds had tacitly consented and in which physicians had become unwitting accomplices. Once I became aware of it, it was easier for me to empathize with their predicament. What a life they were leading!

The Reynoldses did not keep their next appointment. Concerned, I called Mrs. Reynolds at work. She apologized and brought me up to date. Her husband had been admitted to the psychiatric ward of their local hospital. The doctors there diagnosed his condition as "depression" and wanted to begin a round of shock treatments. He refused, went home, restarted his cycle of hospital emergency-room visits, and was admitted to yet another hospital, where, once more diagnosed as having a depressive disorder, he consented to shock treatment.

For these reasons, Mrs. Reynolds said, they had not kept their appointment. Understandable, I thought, also wondering why, given what seemed a positive relationship, they had not sought my services during this time. Why had I not been contacted by any other psychiatrists treating him?

Reflecting on the matter over the next few days, I thought of some possible answers. The Reynoldses were in pursuit of miracles, perpetually seeking that special doctor, the expert more knowledgeable than all the others, who would suddenly discover the root cause of all of Mr. Reynolds's medical problems and cure them. For a brief and shining moment when he was on the medical ward, I was their rescuer and miracle worker. They were impressed with my acumen and regarded his improvement in miraculous terms. Mrs. Reynolds had said as much, and I went along with this. Feeling every bit the hero, I allowed my care and judgment to be clouded by their adulation. I made my diagnosis of depressive disorder without paying enough attention to his history. Then I realized what I should have noticed when he was on the medical ward: his pain had diminished even before I had prescribed the antidepressant.

When Mr. Reynolds's symptoms returned, my Dr. Miracle image was tarnished in their minds and they launched on a search for a new miracle worker. I had erred, and other physicians would as well. Mr. Reynolds would continue to make his appearances in hospital emergency rooms, which would be followed by endless series of appointments with psychiatrists, internists, surgeons—the whole medical profession if need be—in pursuit of a miracle. These new doctors, sure of their own curative powers, were unlikely to contact his previous healers.

Considering this latest go-around, I felt certain that the effects of the shock treatment would be short-lived. I knew that short-term cures were possible in hypochondriasis, the result of the expectation of a miracle and the presence of a perceived miracle worker. I mused—even hoped—that perhaps Mr. Reynolds would return to my office. I still retained the somewhat naive belief that

I could accomplish what others and I had so far failed to do and alleviate the misery of the Reynoldses' lives. I was therefore pleased a few months later when Mr. Reynolds phoned for an appointment and unwittingly lent credence to my hypothesis.

"You helped me once," he said. "Perhaps you can do it again."

This time around, I vowed to be more rigorous in my history taking. When Mr. Reynolds returned to my office, he looked somewhat better, even smiled occasionally, but still barked complaints of pain while gripping his abdomen. As expected, Mrs. Reynolds was the primary source of information.

"When my husband was sixty-two, ten years ago, and had to retire after his heart attack, all he had to do was sit around and worry. You can't blame him for worrying, Doctor. But, you know, I was surprised. He still called the doctors all the time and he still felt a little better when he spoke to them. And then—well, two things happened. He watched a television program about colon cancer. And right after that—immediately—he developed bowel symptoms. He was up half the night—and he kept me up with him."

Mrs. Reynolds's recitation had a familiar ring, but patients often repeat the same stories, adding and subtracting information as they go along. In this instance, what was new was the detail about the television program. I had to wonder if the incidence of phone calls from hypochondriacs to their physicians doesn't skyrocket with each television program about illness or doctors.

She went on, "While he had those symptoms with his bowels, he saw a gastroenterologist, who couldn't find anything. But with my husband, nobody wants to take a chance, you know, so the doctor suggested a procedure where they put an instrument in the rectum to look at the colon."

I noticed that Mrs. Reynolds never referred to her husband by name or used any terms of endearment. In her vocabulary, Mr. Reynolds was "he" or "my husband."

She continued, "While he was having this done, the doctor took a scraping of some tissue, from the colon or somewhere. He sent the tissue to the laboratory for examination. So far, so good. Then the doctor made his mistake. Why can't you doctors be a little more clever? He told my husband there were a few 'suspicious' cells. Why did he have to tell him this? But he"—Mrs.

Reynolds looked directly at her husband—"he went crazy. The doctor was a fool to tell him. What for? So he could become convinced he has cancer? No one can tell him differently. You can't reassure him."

None of this information had appeared in Mr. Reynolds's hospital chart, and he certainly had not volunteered it. But this was not unusual, because hypochondriacs withhold information. I also pondered the gastroenterologist's position. He was caught between the need for full disclosure in an increasingly litigious world and the need to quell the anxieties of his patient. I felt certain that the doctor could not have fully comprehended the significance of his words, because Mr. Reynolds was a new patient. This could have happened with any physician and any diagnosis.

Whatever the case, the gastroenterologist's report set off an irreversible chain of events. Apart from his continual concern about cancer, Mr. Reynolds could no longer be reassured by calls to his numerous physicians. Before the cancer episode, these telephone conversations with his doctors had calmed him down for a while; now, no part of the day was without severe anxiety. Because the Reynoldses were so dependent on doctors for concern and loving care, it becomes easy to understand why they came down so hard on doctors when they felt "failed" or "let down" or a diagnosis was "missed." Mrs. Reynolds corroborated my conclusions when she told me what had happened years ago when her husband noticed that the glands in his groin were swollen. Mr. Reynolds's doctors said the swelling was "nothing" and would soon go down. It didn't and, in fact, turned out to be symptomatic of an infectious disorder that required weeks of hospitalization before it could be brought under control.

"Doctors don't know what they are doing," they said, almost in unison.

Mr. Reynolds had not told me much about himself apart from his medical problems, and I used a pause in the session to ask about other aspects of his history. I asked him about his childhood. What was it like?

As usual, Mrs. Reynolds did the answering. Her replies sounded rehearsed, as though she had offered them many times before. "When he was five, he cut his arm and had a major infection. At seven, he was so badly burned by a charcoal fire, he had to be rushed to the hospital."

Many think that the traumatic events of childhood, especially those involving illness, can trigger a predisposition to hypochondria. In Mr. Reynolds's case, such traumas were abundant.

Jumping ahead to the more recent past—patients rarely relate information in strict chronological order—Mrs. Reynolds told me how, on more than one occasion, he had overdosed—and not just on the tranquilizers and painkillers that made him delirious. There was the time, for example, when Mr. Reynolds had mistakenly taken too many Digoxin, a cardiac medicine, when Mrs. Reynolds had mixed them in a bottle of the painkiller Percodan—accidentally.

Just how accidentally, I silently wondered.

I wondered, too, how Mrs. Reynolds could continue living with this man without harboring violent thoughts against him. How often, if ever, did she think she might be better off without him? If she did, she didn't seem to express her anger and frustration openly. On the other hand, his anger was also well hidden, replaced by constant complaining.

Indeed, it seemed to me as I got to know them better that the Reynolds's system of living together was designed to keep overt anger in check. When the system broke down, "accidental" overdoses were a result. I sensed that their system was firmly entrenched and could not be altered. The best I could hope to do was to keep the system in check and prevent acts of hostility from replacing their current oblique expressions of anger. I decided to do this by supporting Mrs. Reynolds's caring attitude and complimenting her devotion and patience.

I tried to implement what I thought would be a fruitful approach by arranging for Mr. Reynolds to have a doctor familiar with the subtleties of his case serve as a clearinghouse for medical information—a kind of control headquarters. I chose a particularly understanding internist who I knew would respond to the Reynoldses' phone calls and would do a thorough examination at each visit, if not to unearth or confirm some malady, at least to reassure the patient that all was well.

But despite my well-laid plans, Mr. and Mrs. Reynolds saw

this carefully selected internist only once. They realized he was not the miracle worker they had expected; and they didn't return to my office, either.

Six months later, I ran into Mr. Reynolds on the surgical ward quite by chance. He had just had stomach surgery. At this point, I was sufficiently cynical to wonder whether his stomach was really diseased and, out of interest, I read his chart. Indeed, his stomach had been badly diseased. He had a perforated ulcer. I also saw that he had reported excruciating pain prior to surgery. If his complaints had been taken this time as yet another example of his hypochondria, it would have been the kind of incident his doctors had dreaded all along.

I had a pleasant conversation with Mr. Reynolds. At last, he said, he was free of pain. But I suspected that this release would be short-lived. In matters like this, one hopes to be proven wrong.

As I had anticipated, only a few months passed before Mr. Reynolds's name once again appeared on the patient roster. This time, I was called in to see him. The abdominal pain had returned. His physicians now attributed it to a degeneration of the vertebral bones in his lower back, and he had undergone lumbar spine surgery. The surgery had taken care of the pain (only temporarily it turned out), but now Reynolds's legs were paralyzed and he was confined to a wheelchair. He looked wretched and, although he was not a very big man, he seemed cramped and confined in the wheelchair. I called his neurologist, who told me he found no physical reason for his continuing paralysis; I was unable to offer any fresh insights, let alone "miracle cures." In time, however, Mr. Reynolds recovered some use of his limbs (I guess that being in a wheelchair complicated his life more than he had anticipated!) and—unexpectedly—called me for an appointment.

At this session, he walked in supported by his wife and a female companion, who remained in the waiting room. In a reversal of roles, he did the talking while Mrs. Reynolds listened. It was evident that he had something he wanted to share and he proceeded to do so, punching out his sentences in staccato style.

"Doctor, I could always maintain an erection for one hour. I can't get on top of her, Doctor. My back is so bad."

Confronted with this, Mrs. Reynolds began her counterattack. "He always had a problem with orgasm. He would take so long, over an hour. It was painful for me. Now he wants me to get on top of him. It's impossible. I can't be in that position for so long."

It became clearer how their anger influenced their sexual life. He, the overt sufferer, inflicted prolonged and painful intercourse on his wife, the silent sufferer, by withholding his orgasms for so long and making the experience painful for her. But she apparently consented, as long as she did not have to endure the additional discomfort of the superior position for long periods. Now, however, I saw that the system was failing and their anger was being more overtly expressed. She was actively denying him one of his few remaining pleasures. I was pleased to see that, in spite of everything, he was still interested in sex.

I wasn't sure how to respond.

Mr. Reynolds provided the words, continuing his verbal battering with those choppy sentences that I had heard as perseveration and counted as a sign of delirium when I first met him. Now they were weapons, means of expressing the underlying anger I had long been sensing.

"She's hired a woman to stay with me. I'm in terrible pain. There's a lot of things doctors don't find. I'm not good enough for that woman."

He paused and aimed a look at his wife. "My mother was stupid. She pinched me. She hated me. She was vicious. She always took me to doctors. I'm going through hell. For God's sake . . . She's too perfect. The only weakness she has is me." He smiled at me. "I don't like the woman who is staying with me."

I attempted to direct our conversation to what had been happening at home apart from the sexual difficulties. Because of his inability to walk unaided, Reynolds was no longer able to spend time at the local brokerage house. He was totally dependent on his wife, who had, of her own accord, hired the daytime companion. This made matters worse. His symptoms of pain and fears of cancer intensified. The number of his phone calls to Mrs. Reynolds's office increased, as did those to the emergency medical service number. The companion's presence was irrelevant. In his mind, Mrs. Reynolds's act was a hostile one that increased his sense of her unavailability. No wonder Mrs. Reynolds had rejected this advice early on.

The Reynoldses kept two more appointments. At the first, I saw the anger between them surface and show its full force. For each thought that Mr. Reynolds blurted out, Mrs. Reynolds barked a reply.

Their system was not working efficiently, I thought, if all this anger is being expressed so openly. The back disability, sexual difficulties, and presence of the companion—in what way had these contributed to the breakdown of their system?

I don't recall whether what happened next was spontaneous or the result of my prodding, but Mr. Reynolds provided the first detailed glimpse of his childhood. His mother *was* the hateful tyrant to whom he had briefly alluded. She whipped him daily with a cat-o'-nine-tails kept specifically for this purpose, and he showed me the now-faint scars to prove it. He also revealed that it had been his mother who had cut his arm and burned him and that she also forced him to leave the toilet unflushed so that she might inspect his productions for their acceptability. When they weren't, he was immediately rushed to a doctor.

Mr. Reynolds's mother blended a disproportional concern for his health with sadistic behavior. The result of this upbringing was the incorporation of a severe masochistic element into Mr. Reynolds's character, and hypochondria. Although all hypochondriacs possess some self-destructive traits, when they loom as large as they did in Mr. Reynolds's case, their negative influence is profound. As an adult, Mr. Reynolds tortured himself endlessly and brought a substitute mother, Mrs. Reynolds, into his life to both care for and rage at him. He, in turn, became a torturer, venting his pent-up rage on his wife and his other primary care givers—his physicians. Not unusually in cases of masochism, the drive becomes libidinized and attaches to the individual's sexuality. Sexual fantasies involve torture and beating.

I saw Richard Reynolds for the last time a week later, almost two years after our initial encounter. For the first time, his wife was not at his side when the session began, having been unable to find a parking space. Her absence, however, did not inhibit him from talking and he bombarded me with his usual litany of complaints and observations, saying, most interestingly, "The pain brings on my orgasms."

Although I had not been able to make a positive difference to the unhappy lives of Mr. and Mrs. Reynolds, I learned much from seeing them. Generally, I learned how old age influences the severity of hypochondria because of the real specter of physical illness and the stresses accompanying retirement. I saw how hypochondria in old age does not need to be associated with other psychiatric disorders—it can be primary. And I realized, with some irony, that the increased need for physicians by the elderly can worsen the life of a hypochondriac when the patient withholds vital information, when communication between patient and doctor is poor, and when diagnostic errors are made.

More specifically, I saw how easily Mrs. Reynolds was incorporated into a schema that endlessly replayed Mr. Reynolds's childhood relationship with his mother, one that oscillated between caring and sadism. The collusion between husband and wife allowed them to maintain some tranquility, but because the original problems were never confronted, the calm was regularly broken by a storm of new ones. These new problems, in turn, worsened the hypochondria and sometimes were even life threatening.

In the privileged way afforded physicians, I had learned about an individual's life from childhood to old age and the childhood determinants of lifelong hypochondria.

My education also came from observing my own fallibility and limitations. My pride and belief in my own expertise were of no more use than my patient's belief in miracles. Sadly, I had to accept that not all situations are reversible, even in the presence of the most diligent among us. From my experience with Richard Reynolds, I learned that the chances of success with hypochondriacs are exponentially worsened by their ingrained, self-destructive traits, and how these masochistic tendencies become sexually attached and offer the victims a few moments of bliss in an otherwise pleasureless, tortured existence.

·5·

The Man with the Trembling Arm

Peter Pryce-Jones had been in couples' therapy for over a year before he was referred to me for individual treatment. Jane Rosen, the social worker who had treated the Pryce-Joneses, provided some preliminary information. The patient and his wife had sought help because they were fighting incessantly. Jane had seen this as a problem of communication and tried to show Pryce-Jones that escalating his anger at his wife was secondary to his increasing frustration with other aspects of his life and the turns it was taking. He was a public relations executive who no longer found his work particularly fulfilling.

Pryce-Jones had taken to calling in sick or, occasionally, simply not showing up at work. His sexual interest in his wife had never been great, but now it was markedly diminished. His frustrations showed themselves in bursts of anger that his wife matched in intensity. Like the Reynoldses, they were caught in a cycle they couldn't break.

Jane also told me she had discovered that Pryce-Jones had a preoccupation with illness, and she had seen these concerns balloon out of proportion over the year of treatment. She called him a hypochondriac. Nonetheless, confronted with his persistent complaints of pain, fatigue, swelling, and achiness, she referred him to an internist, who gave him a "million-dollar" workup and a prescription for the antidepressant Prozac. Noticing a tremor in one arm, the patient consulted a neurologist, who decided to stop the Prozac.

Unable to make inroads into their problems, the social worker told them it might be more productive if each sought individual therapy. Knowing of my interest in mind/body disorders and sensing that they might be part of Pryce-Jones's problems, she called me to see if I would be willing to take the patient on.

It took about a month for Pryce-Jones to call for an appointment. In the interim, I had not given him much thought—he seemed to be just another patient referred by a colleague who, for one reason or another, perhaps just fear of seeing a psychiatrist, never makes an appointment. This is not unusual in my profession.

"Dr. Goodman?" he asked with an English accent. "Mrs. Rosen told me to see you. When might you be able to see me?" he said, in a condescending tone.

The mention of Mrs. Rosen told me who was calling, and I could not help wondering if the delay and the attribution of responsibility for doing so to another were signs of reluctance on his part. I knew that people preoccupied with concerns about physical illness have a special reluctance to contact psychiatrists. But, no, I would not permit myself to jump to conclusions.

"Is this something pressing?" I always ask this question. Patients are invariably anxious when they call, and asking if the matter is urgent gives them an immediate sense of the doctor's concern.

Pryce-Jones replied, "Not at all. No rush. At your convenience." His Englishness was now very evident.

"I have an opening next Wednesday."

"No, I can't make that. Can you do it on Friday?"

"Yes," I said. "By the way, you haven't given me your name."

He carefully spelled his last name for me, stressing the *y* in "Pryce" and making sure I didn't leave out the hyphen—signs, I would learn, of a man who could be just as precise about other things as well.

Waiting for Pryce-Jones to arrive that Friday, I imagined a Savile Row–tailored gentleman, a candidate for a gin-and-tonic ad, fiftyish, graying at the temples, and thoroughly distinguished-looking. Instead, I met a younger man dressed in Levi's and an open-necked sports shirt, too small to cover a burgeoning paunch. He had a pleasant face, with soft features and red hair that was neatly combed but in need of a trim. When he sat down in the patient's chair and crossed his legs, I noticed that his shoes were badly scuffed. His accent was upper-class English, and when he was under stress, as I would soon hear, it became more pronounced.

When he seemed unable to get past words of greeting, I began, "Mrs. Rosen has told me something about you, but I would rather have you tell me in your own words why you have come here."

"I've really come to see you because my wife and Mrs. Rosen insisted. I do not believe there is anything wrong with me psychologically. My problems are physical. And what's more, I have had them for more than twenty years. Mainly, I have prostatic congestion. I feel like urinating all the time. It can be quite devastating, you know. I worry a lot about my health and small things, too." He did not specify what the small things were. "My hands are swollen in the morning when I get up. Something is wrong with my circulatory system."

I noticed that his complaints did not relate to anything Jane Rosen had told me.

He went on, "Lately, my left arm has been trembling. I am most worried about this. And I get dizzy spells. It all adds up to a neurological condition, I know for sure. You probably won't believe all of this, anyhow. I've never had much faith in the medical profession, and you are part of it. Doctors don't take my symptoms seriously and, believe me, I know. I've seen enough of them."

As he said this, I felt some of the anger that Jane Rosen had told me about.

"I went to see a neurologist. I am sure you know Dr. Martin. He was a little better than most. At least he was able to tell me why my arm was trembling. Some idiot had prescribed Prozac. Dr. Martin said Prozac made my arm shake and told me to stop taking it—immediately. I was relieved to find someone who took my symptoms seriously and knew what the devil he was up to."

In assigning the cause of his trembling arm to Prozac, Dr. Martin managed to relieve the patient's anxiety but unwittingly confirmed his belief that doctors are error prone and hasty to write prescriptions. My inclination was to ask why, if the neurologist was such a hotshot diagnostician, the trembling in his arm had not disappeared. I restrained myself. One doesn't like to criticize another physician in front of his patients, even though this particular neurologist had a reputation for faulting the diagnoses and treatments of his colleagues.

It was rapidly becoming apparent that Jane Rosen was correct when she called him a hypochondriac. For an instant, I reflected on the roles that physicians play in keeping hypochondria alive. What is a hypochondriac without his physicians? Then I reprimanded myself that I was beginning to see myself as better than the other doctors he had seen. I was falling into Pryce-Jones's trap by thinking I was going to succeed where my colleagues had failed. I also noticed that Pryce-Jones had triggered another nonsalutary process: I had begun to feel defensive—and I would feel this way intermittently with Pryce-Jones. He had expressed negative feelings about other doctors. What, I wondered, was in store for me? I must keep my guard up.

"Actually, I don't know what I am doing here," said Pryce-Jones. "I don't know why I let myself get talked into coming here." He shook his head vigorously to register his own disbelief. "I must be crazy. My problems are physical. Do you understand?"

There was a hint of threat in his voice. I thought I was experiencing the militancy of the hypochondriac who needed to fight to maintain his physical symptoms and never reveal the emotional problems underlying them, because he was afraid of experiencing the unpleasant sensations that would accompany their exposure.

"Why were you put on Prozac in the first place?" I asked.

"God knows," he said. "They use that stuff for everything now. I read that in *Ad Age*. Soon as a person says he feels depressed, boom, a prescription for Prozac follows."

"Have you lost any weight?" I asked, beginning a line of questions that test for depressive disorder, which, as I have said, is often a cause of secondary hypochondria.

"Maybe. A little. Not much. Hard to have an appetite when you feel ill."

"How are you sleeping?"

"Fine. I take sleeping pills."

"Have you noticed any change in your mood?"

"Of course! What do you expect when you feel so sick?"

My questioning was cut short when Pryce-Jones decided to return to talk of his physical symptoms. He reviewed his history in an organized, detailed, chronological, and—I noticed—practiced way. I recalled how carefully he had spelled his name for me. Only barely turned forty, for years Pryce-Jones had endured a host of physical symptoms for which definitive causes were never found. He repeated that in his late teens he started having trouble with urination. The problem never went away, and he still felt a constant urge to urinate. He described his response to these symptoms as devastating.

As well it might be in one so young, I thought. A young man in the throes of developing sexual expression and sexual identity inexplicably confronted with the need to urinate twenty or thirty times a day must wonder what is going on in his sexual organs. At age twenty, few of us are anatomical experts. Urination and reproduction are, not surprisingly, linked in many minds.

Pryce-Jones made no allusion to his sexual history, choosing to stay with the purely clinical aspects of his case. He said that the physician he saw, a specialist of some renown (he said), had found he had an inflammation of the prostate, the small gland that, in men, sits where the urethra emerges from the bladder.

"Did you think that something was wrong with you sexually?" I asked.

He missed the connection. "All I cared about was my health. I could think of nothing else."

Later I would learn that Pryce-Jones saw himself as a highly sexual man who was, indeed, preoccupied with his sexual performance. For the moment, however, he remained intent on telling his medical history.

His initial treatment for his prostate was ineffective, and so Pryce-Jones subsequently consulted a number of London specialists. All made the same diagnosis: prostatitis, an inflammation of the gland. All prescribed similar courses of treatment. None, however, provided a cure and, now, innumerable drugs and procedures later, he said, he was still seeing doctors for this condition.

"What precisely do you feel when you have this urge to urinate?" I asked.

Pryce-Jones said there was something heavy between his scrotum and his anus that never went away. Sometimes his urine burned, and sometimes he noticed that the stream was interrupted; it came out in spurts. Sometimes, he said, it took him a full minute before he could initiate urination. He said that he no longer used urinals, preferring stalls, like a woman, because he was embarrassed to stand, unable to initiate urination, next to other men.

His descriptions were detailed and accurate, a classic presentation of the symptoms of prostatitis. Too precise, perhaps. Pryce-Jones seemed too knowledgeable and too schooled and, unlike most patients, he used no vernacular terms. I had my doubts, but was not yet ready to discount the diagnosis of prostatitis. I had known of cases where a diagnosis of hypochondriasis had been made when prostatitis would have been the correct diagnosis.

I thought of John Wright, a forty-nine-year-old who had not worked for years because of severe back pain. To maintain his eligibility for disability, he had to submit to frequent physical examinations. No one had ever made a definitive diagnosis, although "disabilityitis" was often mentioned, and there was a feeling among his physicians and his family that he was a "goof-off." This went on until, by chance, he was sent to the one specialist he had never seen, a urologist. As part of the routine examination, the urologist put his finger into the patient's rectum to feel the prostrate and, in the process, a large amount of pus was passed through Wright's penis. For years, Wright had had an abscess of the prostate without showing any symptoms of this condition, except lower back pain. Once the abscess burst, the pain vanished and the patient resumed a productive life-style. Having been one of Mr. Wright's specialists at one point, this episode left me especially attentive to the possibilities of physical illness in people classified as hypochondriacs.

I now attempted to change the direction of Pryce-Jones's session. "I would like to get to know something about you personally," I said.

He said he had been a journalist in England but went into public relations here and was an executive in a well-known firm. I conjured up an image of an affably persuasive PR man spending his day going from expensive lunches to cocktail parties and dinners, with a few "meetings" in between to sell clients and media on using public relations techniques to advance a cause, personality, or product. I had no doubt that he was an effective PR executive, just as I saw how convincing he could be in a doctor's examining room. Physicians took him seriously but could never cure him. Consequently, he had been forced to go from doctor to doctor in hopes of a correct diagnosis and cure. He had now come to believe, he reiterated, that "Doctors are not as proficient as they would have you believe."

Pryce-Jones's next statement struck me with awe. He said that he (more likely his insurance carrier) had spent more than $32,000 on physicians' fees and tests in the past year alone. "What is more, wouldn't you have emotional problems if you had so many illnesses and no one could treat them? Of course, I am anxious. Of course, I feel depressed."

He said this with an impatience that sent me a signal not to push him on "psychiatric nonsense"—he was not ready to believe any of it. He added that he had been on numerous tranquilizers, which only succeeded in making him tired. The list of drugs that he proceeded to rattle off sounded like a reading of the *Physicians' Desk Reference.*

I said, "I notice you have not said anything about why you and your wife were in treatment with Mrs. Rosen."

The response came quickly. "I never wanted to or needed to be. My wife insisted. She's the unhappy one. Nothing seems to satisfy her. Must be her change of life."

At forty? I wondered.

The session was just about over, and I remember hesitating before suggesting that he return in a week and being surprised when he acquiesced.

Every patient affects the psychiatrist in some way and sets a thinking process in motion. The psychiatrist cannot stop thinking about the patient's problems, and some of his more important work and understanding goes on during the intervisit period. I call this "homework." Pryce-Jones took up a lot of my thinking that first week. I was fairly sure his diagnosis was primary hypochondria. I saw no signs of any other emotional disorder. Moreover, the patient met the criteria: he took any physical sign or sensation as proof of physical illness and had been doing so for most of his life.

Pryce-Jones provided no evidence of having secondary hypochondria: for example, depressive disorder or anxiety disorder associated with somatization symptoms. Everything he related on his first visit confirmed my impression of the patient as someone who had had his symptoms for many years and for whom having these symptoms had became a way of life. But so sure was I of my clinical assessment, I neglected to ask myself some important questions. Pryce-Jones, in turn, was determined to maintain the image of the sufferer whom medical science had failed and, persuader that he was, he was quite forceful in promoting that vision. Only in retrospect did I see that the collusion that resulted between us had derailed me from making an accurate clinical assessment early on.

Pryce-Jones returned angry and disgruntled the following week. "You did not pay enough attention to my physical complaints at our last meeting. Since you're a doctor and not a social worker, I hoped you would have been able to confirm the reality of my physical complaints. I don't know why I came back."

Nonetheless, he had returned and had done so looking quite sad and sloppy. Having completed his scolding, he started to talk about his emotional problems. I was caught off balance.

Pryce-Jones was not happy with his wife; he had never been throughout eighteen years of marriage. He had never wanted children; she did, and they had one. He had wanted a spouse who stayed home and waited for him to return from work each day; she had gone to work. Their sexual relationship had never satisfied him, and he had lost interest in her years ago. Recently, their relationship had gotten worse. He had a long history of extramarital relationships (probably thinking, in part, that sex would alleviate his "dammed up" prostate). All his life, he had loved picking up younger women and was adept at it.

Perhaps he perceived an eagerness on my part to know how he did this or perhaps he had a need to impress me with his superior masculinity. He went on, as Leporello had catalogued Don

Giovanni's exploits, to tell of how he managed to seduce so many young women so successfully. His choice of venue was restaurants. He would start a conversation with a woman sitting alone and then invite her to join him, after which the rest was easy. Like Don Giovanni's, his conquests were many.

Did I believe him? He certainly told his story in a way that dispelled suspicions of fabrication. But then, the Don was convincing, too, until one realized that all of his attempts—in Mozart's opera, at least—were unsuccessful.

As a psychiatrist, I *am* forever looking for opportunities to impute contrary meanings. Was Pryce-Jones, I wondered, impotent with his wife now? He must have read my mind, because he then confessed that the reason he had so much difficulty with his wife was that he was impotent with her. This was the real reason his wife had insisted that they see the social worker Jane Rosen.

I asked myself if he could have major depression, of which impotence is a symptom. Why hadn't this occurred to me at our first meeting? Certain indicators had been there—his casual, almost sloppy dress, for one. I recalled Jane Rosen's statement that his life and job were no longer fulfilling, and I wondered whether this also meant that he was depressed.

Most important, I wondered why one of his latest consultants had started him on the antidepressant Prozac. Had Pryce-Jones told this doctor about his poor appetite and sleeping difficulties (symptoms of depressive disorder)? Why was Pryce-Jones consenting to see me now?

I considered the last question and answered it with more questions. Had something specific happened—at home, at work—so that he was now allowing himself to see a psychiatrist? Was some inner voice telling him that something more than his usual precarious physical state was amiss?

Although I was not yet convinced that he had a depressive disorder, I was fairly certain that this was not a man who would be able to tolerate any probing, let alone a comprehensive examination, of his emotions.

"I think you should take Prozac again," I told him. "It might relieve some of your symptoms. I don't believe the trembling in your arm came from Prozac. If that had been the case, you would have felt the trembling in both arms. Besides, you have told me the trembling was there long before you began taking Prozac and it hasn't gone away now that you have stopped the medication," I said as gently as possible.

"I am not going to take any *psychiatric* medication," he said with a resolve that I had no choice but to accept. He changed the subject and thrust a typed sheet of paper at me. "Read this. Then you'll know what's wrong with me."

I looked at the paper, which I saw was a carefully prepared list of his symptoms and the physicians he had consulted—resembling, in a way, the kind of press release that PR men specialize in. The list included a detailed summary of physical complaints that included: swollen glands every morning; missed heartbeats, all the time; pain in wrists, assumed to be due to carpal tunnel syndrome (a constriction of the median nerve in the wrist) and connected by the patient to a faulty adrenal hormone system; extreme, intermittent skin sensitivity, sometimes so severe that he could not be touched; persistent lower-back pain; trembling in left hand.

He made references to "abnormal firing neurons" and attempted to explain his symptoms in pseudophysiological terms. He also listed the names of many physicians he had consulted. The English names, complete with titles—Sir Adrian Fisher, Sir Alexander Hepworth, Julian Smithers, Sir Reginald Fife-Evans—sounded like a virtual medical Who's Who of London's Harley and Wimpole streets. His American physicians, all with impressive academic titles, were associated with major university hospitals.

I put the document aside. Pryce-Jones kept switching hoops on me, as if this were Wonderland and we were playing croquet in the Red Queen's garden. One moment, he was talking about his personal life; the next, he was listing his physical complaints. He did not make these moves consciously. Instead, his mind was responding to a perceived threat, perhaps the possibility that his disorders might indeed be emotional. An unconscious effort was being made to take me off the scent of a psychiatric diagnosis.

The hour ended with his refusal to accept a prescription for Prozac and his acceptance of an appointment time for the following week. On my part, I promised to give his list a thorough going-over. When I did, I saw how much and how little Pryce-

Jones had revealed about himself and his malady on that single page. He had a thorough style and was not one to omit details. The details confirmed what he had already told me—that he was a worrying type of hypochondriac. This may sound odd; aren't all hypochondriacs worriers? Yes, but to different degrees. Some worry less within themselves and complain more to others. Others are manipulators who use their symptoms to make friends and relatives do their bidding. They promote guilt feelings by shifting the responsibility for their symptoms onto others. For some, dependence on other people is paramount, and they will do or say anything to achieve this end. There is a considerable overlapping of these personality traits, and any one of them can predominate at a given time. Thus, personality styles influence the expression of hypochondria and how the individual communicates his psychological predicaments in physical language.

The more I reviewed the list, the more I realized how odd his symptoms were. None made complete sense from a diagnostic point of view. Medicine is, after all, both a science and a very logical craft. A physician grows accustomed to hearing certain symptoms over and over again; they form a pattern. But Pryce-Jones's symptoms seemed merely an approximation of clinical symptoms. For example, pain is distributed in patterns determined by the anatomical paths of the nervous system, and his pain did not follow those paths.

In his case, so many symptoms had affected so many parts of his body for so many years without being substantiated by tests or responding to the ministrations of so many well-known specialists that I had to question whether their origins were physical. Without a doubt, Pryce-Jones's hands were actually swollen in the morning. But such swelling is not uncommon, especially in those who happen to sleep with their hands and arms underneath their bodies. Similarly, the trembling in his arm was real. But because it occurred only in one arm, it might have been ascribable to a habit of holding a phone very tightly—something a PR man might do.

Pryce-Jones's observations were not faulty. While hypochondriacs have an extremely heightened awareness of bodily sensations, it is what they attribute them to that sets them apart. Sure that his body sensations were symptoms of illness, Pryce-Jones made his life an endless round of consultations, testing, explanations (doctors are scientists and require explanations as much as their patients do), and treatment.

Pryce-Jones's list, as well as his speech, reflected a mastery of medical terminology and information—almost, but not quite. Scrutinizing his list, I noticed juxtapositions that did not make sense; this made them revealing. For example, adrenal hormone has nothing to do with carpal tunnel syndrome. His "press release" had done little more than confirm my suspicion of hypochondria. But what about the presence of an associated emotional disorder? I had observed some signs of depressive disorder, but I needed to see more.

Pryce-Jones loved women, or so he said. Yet he had been unable to make love to his wife for some time, and even in the more remote past, they had not been entirely compatible sexually. He preferred the sexual company of the nameless women he regularly picked up in restaurants and elsewhere. The fact that he proudly relayed this information registered in my memory. In the early years of my training, I had treated a handsome fourteen-year-old who regaled me with stories of his sexual conquests. They were so interesting and so complete, I became more absorbed in them than I should have. My supervisor, with whom I discussed the case, had to prod me back to reality. He did so with the simple question: "Do you think he may be exaggerating?"

I opened my next session with Pryce-Jones by asking, "Are you still having those casual sexual encounters you described at our first meeting?"

If he answered yes, I had reason to assume that he was impotent only with his wife. But he hedged. There was a long pause before he answered. After all, he had gone to great lengths to establish his masculine credentials and I was, in essence, asking for a refutation.

"No, I haven't been pursuing those women of late. I haven't felt well enough to."

Exactly, I thought. Hypochondriacs always hide behind their symptoms, and Pryce-Jones had given me the clue I needed while at the same time protecting his virile image. His sexual desire was unquestionably diminished or even absent. I had unearthed another sign of depressive disorder.

Predictably, he changed the subject. "I'm getting older. I've always had an enormous fear of this. The illnesses have just increased my fears of dying. Old age is just going to bring more and more illness. My profession is one for young people. Public relations pushes you out when you are in your forties. I know I am being edged out."

"Has anyone at work actually said this?"

"No. No one ever said this. But I know it is the truth." Pryce-Jones said he had been trying to give his life another direction. "This will take time. I've really been under enormous pressure—stress, you know."

I realized then that what Pryce-Jones was presenting as stressors may actually have been the expression rather than the cause of a depressive disorder. He had not offered any evidence to support his notion that his life in public relations was drawing to a close. Depressive disorder forces one to view the world in the most pessimistic terms and come to believe that one's life is running down inexorably. Reality is diminished. On the other hand, stress can and does exacerbate hypochondria.

Unwittingly, Pryce-Jones had provided me with the chance to pursue the psychological. I concurred that there were indeed many stresses in his life, and I told him that his bodily concerns would always intensify at moments like these. I said, "It is only natural that you feel more afraid and sicker in the face of so many changes at work. We know that for people who tend to express their emotions through physical symptoms, stress is a big factor. We also know that under these conditions, many people give special meaning to any physical changes they feel or observe. Those special meanings are out of proportion to anything real and are read as signs of serious medical illness."

"I had a dream," he said, surprising me at not having beaten his usual retreat to the safe repetition of twitches and itches. In his dream, someone had tried to stab him in his arm and shoulder. That was all he volunteered.

"Was there anything more to your dream?" I asked.

"No." He said nothing more and beat a quick retreat to talk of his prostate condition. However, I knew that the dream might later provide important insight into the nature of his trembling arm.

By now, I was having trouble listening to detailed descriptions of his medical problems. I was irritated. He would arouse my interest in the psychological aspects of his life and then drop the subject. His avoidance of what was extremely unpleasant for him became irksome for me. My reaction was not unusual. The same response can be found in those who live with severe hypochondriacs, whose ranting provokes feelings of helplessness and extreme frustration—a response usually met with accusations of betrayal and not caring. The outcome of what becomes a behavioral cycle is a battered and bewildered family member asking the doctor "How do we talk to him? Are we being too harsh?"

My response was to interject that I found ample evidence to suggest a psychiatric problem, an error I compounded by adding, "I don't feel psychotherapy will be of use to you as long as you concentrate on your physical symptoms." I had confronted the patient with a truth, in this case that his problems were emotionally based. Such a move often leads the patient rapidly to refute the physician's opinion and become further entrenched in the notion that "it's physical."

Pryce-Jones became angry and said with a stiffened resolve that I should have anticipated, "I am not going to take any medicine."

I said no more, grateful that it was the end of the session and I could safely retreat to an analysis of my responses to this patient that would allow me to assume a more constructive approach. Psychiatrists must continually evaluate their responses if their own conflicts are not to intrude on the treatment. My irritation with Pryce-Jones's insistence on reiterating his medical symptoms should not have shown itself. Fortunately, most psychiatric patients are forgiving, but I did not want to test Pryce-Jones's limits of acceptance.

Doing my homework that week, I saw that despite all my mental gyrations, I continued to think of Pryce-Jones as a hypochondriac, without a secondary diagnosis of depressive disorder. By failing to distinguish between primary and secondary hypochondria, I was a specialist responding like a layman who believes that all hypochondria is the same. Pryce-Jones was a master. I understood why he was, despite his fears, a successful public relations man. He had developed a style that kept people ever so slightly off balance, unsure of themselves and unsure of him. He also was the typical hypochondriac, adept at keeping families and physicians perpetually on edge and fearful they may be missing something important. In my office, Pryce-Jones allowed only hints of emotional disorder, just enough to keep me guessing as to what his exact diagnosis might be and always slightly unsure that it wasn't something else.

I continued to hedge a diagnosis of depressive disorder. I still did not have as much evidence as I felt necessary to make a definitive diagnosis, and I could not disregard the long history of primary hypochondria. Nonetheless, I managed to persuade the patient to give Prozac another try. My reward for this was a session of complaints about me, the medication, and its side effects (in most cases, minor and inconsequential). He said that the Prozac made him sleepy and weak, that I only wanted to give him medicine, that I wasn't paying attention to his physical complaints, and that I wanted to label him as mentally ill.

Hardly the case. While medication has become an integral and important part of much psychiatric treatment, it is not dispensed like candy, without detailed instructions and discussions of possible side effects and careful monitoring. Once prescribed, the dosage must be regulated so that the patient receives the maximum benefit from the medication. In this case, I had urged a trial of Prozac because I was paying attention to Pryce-Jones's physical complaints. I knew that hypochondriacs, with their heightened body awareness, do not read side effects as side effects but as signs of new physical illness. I also think that they equate medicine with magic, evoking in them fears of rapid cures. In any case, I did not want to label Pryce-Jones as mentally ill.

Pryce-Jones did not accept my explanations. I knew he was still making the rounds of his specialists, and I began to receive phone calls from them. He had insisted that they ask why I was prescribing Prozac and whether it would interfere with their treatment. He provoked his urologist into asking me whether Prozac affects the prostate. His hand surgeon asked if Prozac gave hand tremors. His dermatologist wanted to know if the drug would make his skin more sensitive. His pharmacist called to see if I had put down the correct dosage. Then his dentist asked if it was all right to give him Novocain. I said, yes. Pryce-Jones didn't believe the dentist and proceeded to track me down and have me paged while I was seeing a patient on the medical wards. He had to hear it himself. Could he take Prozac and have a Novocain injection? "Yes!" I just about screamed into the phone. I had to answer his calls. I was caught in the hypochondriac's web. What if some medication he was taking was incompatible with the Prozac?

Typically, his hearing was selective. I had to repeat instructions over and over in ever-increasing detail. No matter how thorough I was, he always called back, repeating the same questions and adding new ones. He responded to my instructions and advice in a vague and general way. "I'm quite confused," he would say, innocently. I was seeing firsthand how these patients infuriate and alienate their physicians while managing to keep the vital relationship going.

Every so often, he allowed me an emotional pearl. He was not happy. He hadn't made it at work or in life. Others, in his esteem less gifted, had done much better and were making much more money. He had no control over anything . . . the world . . . his family.

He came to the next session and said, "I'm in bad shape."

"What is the matter?"

"My sixteen-year-old son. He told me something very upsetting the other day. Before he told me, he said, 'Dad, I know this is going to make you sweat.' "

I knew that Pryce-Jones had a son, but I knew nothing about the child. I leaned forward and waited for him to continue.

"My son said he thought he was gay. I sweated, all right. He said he was walking down the street and had glanced at men's buttocks. He knew for certain that he had to be gay."

A pause in our conversation allowed me to contemplate this revelation and make some sense of the incident.

"Do you see any similarities here between your son and you?" I asked.

No answer. A slight shrug of the shoulders.

"His style is just like yours. He noticed something virtually in passing and immediately began to imbue it with great significance. He certainly did make you sweat." I stopped there, choosing not to make the next point—that Pryce-Jones, Sr., also had a well-developed talent for making people "sweat."

My analysis was sufficient, however, to evoke a telling of some childhood memories. He told me that he had been a stutterer as a child and had interpreted the stuttering as a sign of his anger. "I was an angry kid. I was always getting into fights. I went to public school [the English equivalent of private school] and in the dormitories—large, open rooms filled with cots—there were always fights among the boys, especially at night when no masters were present. I once hit another boy. I really bloodied him up. I never hit anyone again after that. I got into other fights. Boys will be boys, you know. But I never hit back. I ducked. I was afraid of my power . . . of my anger."

"Are you left-handed?" I asked.

"How did you know?"

I was excited. I remembered his dream, the one in which someone tried to stab him in the arm and shoulder. Pryce-Jones had given me a precious piece of information that I needed to piece his story of the trembling arm together.

"I wonder whether you understand your dream now?"

"What do you mean?"

"Ever since you bloodied that schoolmate's nose, I would venture to say that much of your mental life has been directed to finding a safe way of expressing anger. This was anger you were afraid of and unable to communicate in a rational and acceptable way. In your dream, others were stabbing you. But it was your dream. You made it up. Putting it in the context of what you have told me, however, I think it clearly represented your need to hit others as well as your sense of physical vulnerability. Your fears of anger might stem from the intolerable physical sensations this emotion arouses. Your solution is to express the anger in physical terms. Your more powerful arm, the left, symbolizes your power, your anger. Your hitting arm, rather than hitting, as it did as a child, trembles with rage."

Pryce-Jones did not respond with anger, as I thought he might. He remained unusually quiet and pensive.

I continued, "I don't wish to imply this is all there is to your emotional problems. Far from it. If that were the case, we would all have the same problems as you because we all have angry feelings that are not perfectly channeled and controlled." I told him that he was probably born with a particular susceptibility to expressing his emotional states in physical terms.

I said, "My guess would be, your upbringing influenced and reinforced this solution. I wonder if your parents expressed their emotions in physical terms? It would be nice if we could talk about your parents and childhood in our next session."

Peter Pryce-Jones arrived at his sixth and what was to be his last session displaying an invigorated sense of self. His hair had been trimmed and styled. He wore a pin-striped suit and well-polished black shoes. He strutted in with a certain exaggerated masculine air and was chattier than usual, conforming more to the image I had formed after our initial phone conversation than the man I had been seeing over the past few weeks.

"Nothing has changed," he said as if to dash any hopes I had that he might be feeling better. "I still have my symptoms."

"Which ones?"

"I'm still dizzy when I bend over, and my hands are still swollen in the morning. There has been no change, no change whatsoever, in my prostatic condition."

"What about the trembling in your left arm?"

He looked at his arm as if he had forgotten that it had ever given him any cause to worry, but said nothing.

Although he would not concede change, I knew he had returned to his former self, the primary hypochondriac with his panoply of symptoms. I also knew he had improved remarkably and was probably only vaguely aware that there had been a marked diminution of his physical symptoms and a big improvement in his mood state.

He had been taking Prozac for nearly three weeks, about the time this drug needs to have its effect. Was he better because of Prozac? I thought so. The amount of psychological work we did together was too small to achieve such a marked result so soon. Pryce-Jones was better because he had a depressive disorder and the antidepressant medication had been effective. Although I had treated him with an antidepressant, I had really concentrated on the psychology of his hypochondriacal symptoms and minimized the importance of the evidence that pointed to the concomitant depression that had infinitely worsened the condition and exaggerated the symptoms.

I asked him if he had any thoughts about the previous session. He said no, but I sensed that our discussion was not without impact. I had dared to approach and illuminate the emotional discomfort he worked so hard to distance himself from and hide from others. I felt that it might take a long time for Pryce-Jones to completely absorb and assimilate this information.

"I have decided to terminate this treatment," he announced. "It is costing too much."

This was not his first grumbling about the cost of treatment; his major medical insurance made little allowance for office psychiatric treatment. The irony of the total of his medical expenses compared to my fees had always been lost on him.

"Besides, you haven't helped me all that much," he added, true to style and for good measure.

·6·

The Anxious Attorney

In May 1980, Arthur Walker hurried into my office, headed almost instinctively for the patient's chair, and slumped into it. Fidgety and obviously nervous, Walker launched into the saga of his psychiatric past, which, along with other details of his life, would slowly unfold, monthly meeting after monthly meeting, over the next three years.

During this time, I came to appreciate the importance of diagnosis and the progress that the psychiatric profession has made in fine-tuning diagnostic criteria and improving treatment modes. Had psychiatrists had their present diagnostic capabilities when Walker was initially told that he had a "psychiatric" illness, the pain he endured would have been much less and the course of his life significantly altered.

Arthur Walker had a condition called generalized anxiety disorder (GAD), a frequently found disorder that may not be diagnosed frequently enough. After all, anxiety is ubiquitous and pervasive. On the one hand, medical conditions, such as an overactive thyroid, often trigger anxiety, just as drinking too much coffee may. On the other hand, anxiety accompanies exposure to frightening situations and almost always accompanies emotional illness. More important, no one among us is immune to the effects of stress on our daily lives.

In fact, given anxiety's omnipresence, GAD can be difficult to pinpoint and substantiate as a distinct diagnostic category. Its sufferers may report symptoms like a continual state of muscle tension, feelings of being constantly keyed up and edgy, shakiness, achiness, restlessness, easy fatigability, shortness of breath, palpitations, sweaty palms, dry mouth, dizziness, nausea, diarrhea, flushes or chills, frequent urination, and trouble swallowing—any of which, alone or in combination, persist for at least six months or, more often, many years.

GAD victims agonize over their performances at work, home, or just about everywhere and have an uncertain or negative vision of their future. No explanations of their feelings relieve the anxiety, however professional the source and whatever the logic or scientific evidence. Moreover, they show an array of somatization complaints and are apt to be chronically preoccupied with the state of their hearts, lungs, and digestive tracts. GAD is a cause of secondary hypochondria. Equally as common in men as in women, GAD usually fully manifests itself in people's twenties and thirties. Once diagnosed, it is treatable.

The internist who referred Arthur Walker to me did not suspect GAD. He had been treating Mr. Walker for hypoglycemia and irritable bowel syndrome since 1975 and now suspected that his patient was developing a dependence on Serax, a potentially habituating tranquilizer. The doctor had initially prescribed Serax because he perceived a high level of anxiety in Walker attributable to his patient's physical illness.

Mr. Walker now required increasing amounts of Serax before the desired calming effect was achieved, and the potential for serious withdrawal symptoms existed if the Serax were suddenly stopped. The internist referred him to an expert on drug addiction. After evaluating the patient, this specialist sent a report (later forwarded to me) stating that the patient was adamant about his need for Serax, claiming that without it he felt shaky and unable to function. The report included a summary of Walker's psychiatric history, the recommendation that he see a psychiatrist, and a note that Walker was reluctant to follow this advice.

Confronted with his need for Serax prescriptions, Walker finally bowed to the pressure and consented to a psychiatric consultation. Although he was slumped in my office chair, I could see that he took care with his appearance. I also noticed that his forehead, creased in a perpetual frown, betrayed anxiety that went beyond the usual first-visit jitters. I barely had time to consider his appearance before he began a recitation of his psychiatric history. It was as though the telling of this history was his form of introduction.

In fact, Arthur Walker's psychiatric history did emerge as the most startling aspect of his case. Apart from the abrupt and pressured rendition offered at our initial meeting and the abbreviated summary in the drug expert's report, it was a tale that would thread through our monthly sessions, lending unity and meaning to his life. Moreover, Walker's version would be enhanced and authenticated by the records I was allowed to obtain from a residential psychiatric institution in California where he had spent two late-adolescent years.

Walker began at what he felt was the beginning, dating his symptoms to 1968, when he was eighteen and had left his home in Los Angeles to attend college in Provo, Utah. (Leaving home to go to college can be one of the most stressful events we experience in our lifetimes, and so the time of onset of Walker's symptoms came as no surprise.)

"I smoked pot one evening. Everybody was doing it. You couldn't go to college, even in Utah, and not smoke pot." Agitated, he went on, "Everybody thought pot was harmless. But it wasn't to me. I took a few puffs; I don't think I even inhaled that deeply. Then, all of a sudden, I felt that nothing was real. I was not real. I'll never forget that rush in my brain. I thought I was through. But I reassured myself that it was only the pot. It would soon go away. It didn't. Every day I felt the rush in my brain. I wanted to live, but I didn't want to live. I couldn't deal with life. The pain of living was too much. I just wanted to sleep . . . to escape."

The experiences Walker described—the feeling that his body and surroundings were not real—are known as depersonalization and derealization and are accompanied by an unusual amount of anxiety. Such episodes are fairly common and, when experienced only occasionally, need not be considered abnormal. Walker, however, reported having them daily, although he never again smoked marijuana. These episodes, in fact, became so serious that a university physician decided that he should be admitted to the psychiatric ward of the local hospital. After two weeks of treatment, which included Thorazine, a major tranquilizer, Mr. Walker was released. Returning to campus, he was unable to concentrate or make friends. He and his advisor decided that he could not realistically remain at college, and Walker returned home to Los Angeles, where he continued psychiatric treatment.

The Los Angeles psychiatrist tried many tranquilizers, but Mr. Walker complained that they made him feel like a "zombie" and did not lessen his anxiety. He was so anxious and so depressed about his inability to be helped that he consulted another psychiatrist, who decided he would benefit from a course of electroshock therapy, a treatment usually reserved for people with severe forms of depressive disorder. Fearful but desperate, he submitted to the shock treatment. Six of them. They did not help, and symptoms continued.

Walker remained at home for the rest of the year. His symptoms never went away, although they would occasionally diminish in intensity. Meanwhile, he continued to take the tranquilizers his psychiatrist was prescribing. Once, while taking Haldol, a strong tranquilizer similar to Thorazine, he experienced one of its most frightening side effects. His eyes rolled up into his head, his neck twisted and contorted, and his tongue thickened, making speech difficult. Fortunately, these conditions were reversible, but I had no trouble imagining how this twenty-year-old, already overburdened with anxiety, must have felt while this was happening.

What did Arthur's parents think of all this? How were they involved in his psychiatric treatment? How did his mother and father feel about the shock treatments, about the heavy tranquilization? Because he maintained the strictest control over the information he was prepared to divulge, the answers to these nagging questions were slow in coming.

Arthur returned to Utah and college that fall, after his anxiety had moderated somewhat. He felt an obligation to try. But although he saw a psychiatrist on campus, before long his symptoms returned and, in fact, worsened. He started to feel suicidal. He could not eat; he lost weight; he slept poorly, if at all. Although he said that he felt only very anxious and not seriously depressed, the physicians on hand viewed him as sufficiently depressed to warrant admission to a state mental hospital, where he underwent another series of shock treatments. Walker did not remember how many treatments he received, only that they made no difference.

His doctors recommended that he go to an institution for emotionally disturbed young people not far from San Francisco. In this sheltered environment, he could receive intensive psychotherapy and support while adjusting to being away from his home and family. For Walker, the decision to follow this counsel was fateful.

By now, he had an image of himself as unhealthy. Not surprisingly, he saw himself as mentally ill and the "benefactor" (his word) of inept psychiatric care. These perceptions were so entrenched that all the rehabilitative work attempted when he was in the institution could not restore a healthy sense of self.

While his self-esteem remained severely impaired, his anxiety lessened in the protective and supportive environment of the institution. He was able to venture out of its confines and became more independent. Ultimately, with the encouragement of the institution staff, who recognized his intellectual abilities, he applied to and was accepted at a prestigious California university. Although he experienced frequent and intense episodes of anxiety at college, he forced himself to attend classes and do his assigned work, and graduated.

"I went to law school after graduation. It was hard, but I managed," he said and then skipped ahead to the present—psychiatrists' patients not being subject to demands for orderly presentations of their lives. "Now I work for a large corporation. I'm an in-house counsel. I'm involved in all sorts of business deals. I've had a number of jobs since I left law school, each one slightly more challenging. But too many of my job moves have been lateral rather than upward. I'm still a junior executive. Talk about disappointment."

This emphasis on the negative and distorted self-image was to remain for a considerable portion of his treatment with me and probably will never fully disappear. A poor self-image had

dogged him everywhere for the past twelve years, and he had ex-
pended huge amounts of energy to hide what he thought everybody knew about him—that he was a mental cripple.

"It is obvious they know what's going on," he said, referring
to no one in particular but everyone with whom he came in con-
tact. "Anyone who looks at me can tell that I'm not all right, that
I am liable to go to pieces at any time. If I feel anxious at work,
I disappear . . . leave the office . . . go to the bathroom. I can feel
my heart pounding. Sometimes I think my heart will run away
with itself. My mouth gets so dry, I have to drink and drink.
Sometimes there's a lump in my throat and I can't swallow. Then
I get nauseous . . . feel like vomiting. It gets embarrassing when
I run to the bathroom the whole day. My hands sweat so much,
the paper I'm writing on gets wet. I am sure this is the result of
my hypoglycemia and irritable bowel syndrome."

Mr. Walker spent a large part of his day caring for his hypoglycemia and irritable bowel syndrome (both somatization symptoms). "I try to control my diet to fix my hypoglycemia. I eat
small meals all day long and it helps, although I have to take
small packages of food to work and keep them in my desk. I
know my hypoglycemia is really the cause of all my anxieties."

At our first encounter, Arthur Walker said that he had been
seeing his internist about these conditions for almost five years
and that he preferred seeing him to me. His experience with the
psychiatric profession had made him wary.

"All I want from you is my Serax," he told me as the session
ended. "I am running out of it. If I don't have it, I'll become a
basket case. I can't afford to let that happen. But I don't want,
repeat, I don't want psychotherapy. I don't need it and I don't
want it. I'm only here because *he* wants you to prescribe the
Serax. Otherwise, believe me, I would not be here."

I realized that I would have to prescribe this medicine until I
could arrive at a definite diagnosis. Clearly, Walker was very
anxious and had been that way for so long, it would have been
unfair and wrong clinically if I withheld the Serax at this stage.
Stopping the medication suddenly could have meant withdrawal
symptoms and increased anxiety. I wrote a prescription for seven
days of Serax.

Walker studied the form and said, "This is for a week. I can't come back here next week. I'll lose my job. I must have a month's supply."

I altered the prescription.

Doing my homework, certain aspects of this case became clear. Arthur Walker was presenting only two aspects of himself, and both loomed large. First, there was his "mental handicap," which he wore like a badge. The other was his need for Serax; the tranquilizer had become his life preserver.

But the Serax was helping him. I realized that my initial decision to prescribe only a week's supply had been influenced by the circumstances of his referral; I had sensed his doctor's reluctance to continue prescribing it. Although the drug may indeed be habituating, Serax is also an effective treatment for anxiety disorder, and treatment benefits take precedence provided that the patient's progress can be monitored and control over the prescription maintained.

I reflected on the content of the first session. Walker had related almost nothing but his psychiatric history. I noticed that he wore a wedding band, but he had not mentioned a wife or allowed me the opening to ask about her or whether they had children.

I thought that if he returned to my office, his treatment would have to take two directions. He would need the Serax, and I would have to prescribe it. I also would need to rebuild his self-esteem by slowly redefining his past in more factual terms. I suspected that his previous treatment had been excessive and that although he did have an anxiety disorder, he was not at all a mental cripple. Medication could control the anxiety. I would also have to help him understand that seeing a psychiatrist at this point could benefit him rather than reinforce his self-image as a mental invalid. These were no small tasks, and I was not even sure he would call for another appointment. After all, he could obtain Serax from just about any doctor in the New Jersey suburb he had given as his address.

I also had some thoughts about hypoglycemia and irritable bowel syndrome, two conditions my patients often discuss. These terms seem to encompass a variety of ills for which no conclusive physical findings exist and for which there seem to be no specific remedies.

Patients diagnosed as having hypoglycemia have a wide range of symptoms, from exhaustion to anxiety to sleeplessness to suicidal thoughts. These symptoms can be ascribed to many illnesses, both physical and psychiatric, including generalized anxiety disorder. In some books, hypoglycemics tell how this condition can turn a balanced person into a psychiatric wreck and urge fellow suffers to ignore the results of blood tests that report normal blood sugar values and search for physicians (or osteopaths, chiropractors, or food faddists) who "believe in this condition." Hypoglycemia means low blood sugar. We all can experience its effects if we do not eat for a prolonged period; when we eat, the symptoms disappear. It is doubtful that hypoglycemia is an illness but, if it were, it should respond to measured sugar intake.

Irritable bowel syndrome is associated with a variety of emotional disorders and GAD. It is the most common gastrointestinal "disorder" encountered by primary-care physicians. Its symptoms are an altered frequency of bowel movement, altered consistency of stool, difficulty with the actual passing of stool, and bloating of the abdomen.

Because of the extent of the associated anxiety, I gravitated to psychiatric diagnoses and ran through the gamut of possibilities. I took it for granted that Walker had been tested for every medical condition that might account for his anxiety. But treating hypoglycemia with diet and irritable bowel syndrome with antispasmodic medications had not worked. It was evident that his anxiety was so deeply ingrained and had existed for so long that it could not be easily related to specific, singular events, although it might have been exacerbated by recent stresses the patient had not discussed. His symptoms, of course, did fit into a diagnosis of generalized anxiety disorder with secondary hypochondria.

Still uncertain as to whether he would return, I nonetheless reviewed Walker's records from California that had been forwarded to me. The institution's psychiatrists did not think Walker had depressive disorder. Rather, their studies suggested a diagnosis of psychoneurosis, meaning a disorder that was not psychotic. In light of the understanding of the time, their diagnosis was indeed accurate; generalized anxiety disorder was not yet a recognized diagnosis. Consequently, at that time, Walker never received a trial of the more recently introduced antianxiety medications, which might have ameliorated his symptoms and changed his life early on.

The time I spent doing my homework seemed for naught when Walker phoned to say he did not want to see me again. "What I want is someone who will prescribe my Serax. I do not need a psychiatrist."

"I do not do that," I told him emphatically. "I do prescribe medication but I do not prescribe or renew prescriptions blindly. I need to see the patients I have on medicine regularly to assess what is going on with them. When I give medicine, I assume a responsibility for you. Medications have side effects that must be evaluated. Writing prescriptions is easy; knowing what to write them for is a more complicated matter. I think you should see someone now to get a better idea of what is really wrong with you—especially after all you have been through. I also feel you need treatment to develop a better image of yourself, to build your self-esteem."

I deliberately left this assertion for the end, and even then I had my doubts about having mentioned it. Seeing yet another psychiatrist was liable to reinforce his image of being mentally impaired. Rather than increasing his self-esteem, this might decrease it. That is why I suggested he see me only once a month, a condition to which he agreed. With this compromise, he could think he was seeing me only for medication and spare himself the admission that he needed psychotherapy to repair his damaged self-esteem. For my part, I would know that I might, slowly and gently, be able to reach him without further injuring his already battered ego. I was careful throughout to avoid using the word *psychotherapy.*

Arthur Walker accepted this compromise and came to my office monthly for almost three years. At our meetings, he offered only fragments of personal information at a time. One of his initial revelations, about six visits into his treatment, was that he had recently married and his wife was pregnant with their first child. Clearly, these were the stressors that had worsened his condition and prompted him to seek further help, although in the roundabout style he had adopted to deny psychiatric illness.

Through the remaining months of her pregnancy and even after the baby was born (he did mention that), he rarely spoke of his home life.

If he spoke of a life other than his medical one, it was his professional life. Preoccupied with the direction his career was taking, always certain he was just on the verge of being fired, "What if . . . ?" became the recurrent theme of his sessions. "What if my boss notices that I am crazy?" "What if my boss catches me eating all those little meals?" "What if I can't concentrate?" "What if I get so anxious I can't do my work?" The litany of "what ifs" was endless.

In truth, if his boss or anyone else at the office noticed anything out of line or remarkable about Mr. Walker's behavior, they never shared these observations or criticized him. In fact, I would later learn that he was a valued employee.

When the workday ended, a time Mr. Walker welcomed, he returned home where he said he felt less anxious and more secure. When, at my urging, he finally described his wife, it was with considerable reticence and a genuine reluctance to provide detail. No one found fault with his wife. She was someone everyone loved. She was a landscape architect. In fact, she was a "wonderful" landscape architect and now, having stopped work with the birth of their child, she was a "wonderful" mother.

Over the years, I have noticed that many GAD patients idealize their spouses. Magnifying the positive attributes of their partners may be a partial response to their own feelings of inferiority. I have also noticed that spouses often enter into an unspoken partnership to become enablers, offering sympathy and support and encouraging visits to doctors and other practitioners. In Walker's case, there was a nuance. He never said that *he* thought she was "perfect." This was the pronouncement of others. I also made a mental note that he never boasted about his son, as most new fathers do.

Most of our meetings were dominated by the retelling of his psychiatric history and enumeration of his physical complaints. My role was to provide comments, elucidate, and add detail. I repeatedly pointed out that he felt he had not received proper treatment early on. I told him that as a teenager, events had conditioned him to accept the negative perception of Arthur Walker as "mental cripple" and now he was perpetuating that image. I did not interrupt to correct him or to tell him that I thought his anxiety was part of a psychiatric condition—GAD—although I was convinced this was so. I emphasized that taking Serax for anxiety was appropriate in his case. In fact, I focused on his medication and adjusted its dosage.

In time, Walker's anxiety receded and his workday was no longer the horror it had been. He was less irritable and more relaxed with his boss. It seemed to me that even the creases in his forehead that I initially noticed were smoothing out. Still, there were many rough spots. He adamantly maintained he had hypoglycemia and dismissed suggestions to the contrary. More often than not, I listened to long-winded explanations of hypoglycemia, why he was susceptible, and what he was doing to control it.

Interestingly, he dwelled on his sole marijuana experience and persisted in placing it at the source of his anxiety. He did this in spite of all the events that had transpired since the onset of his symptoms and his awareness on an intellectual level that the drug could not have been the culprit.

It is not unusual for patients and their families to cling to the notion that a drug has caused severe emotional problems. In the sixties, when LSD and mescaline were fashionable, psychotic episodes were often attributed to them, although the symptoms of the psychoses persisted long after the drugs had been stopped.

In fact, it took nearly eighteen months before I could sense that Mr. Walker had established confidence in me. He showed this when he began to disclose more about himself. He devoted a session to a detailed depiction of one of the physical symptoms he had been experiencing for about fifteen years, his constant bouts of constipation and gas, confiding this preoccupation with his bowel.

After detailed complaints about constipation and gas, he hurried on, barely pausing to take a breath: "As long as I am awake, I have pain of varying severity. The pain is always there. Down below the belt, that is where the pain is. At times, the pain gets very severe right at the belly button level—especially if I push in there. I feel horribly bloated. Sometimes the pain radiates into my armpits and all throughout my chest area."

He stopped to take a breath but quickly resumed his monologue. "And then something even worse. I noticed that the consistency of my stool was like toothpaste. Once in a blue moon, it isn't. But it is not necessarily any better when it isn't. It's not an indication of relief. I started to wipe myself but couldn't get myself adequately clean."

I asked what was wrong with the texture of his stool.

"It's a sign something is terribly wrong," he answered. "It is not supposed to be like that. Something is wrong with my bowel. I don't care what the doctors say. It is also messy. I can't take it anymore. It takes me forty-five minutes to wipe myself, it's so messy."

I seized the opportunity and said, "When you first experienced those stomach cramps and had to sit on the toilet for such a long time, sensing you had not completely emptied your bowel, you really were experiencing a common phenomenon that might have come as a response to some emotional stresses. It is not unusual for people to have bowel irregularities as an expression of some emotional circumstance. I am sure you have heard the old expression 'I was so frightened I could have filled my pants.'

"What you did was not so extraordinary, particularly for someone like you who is so aware of what is taking place in your body. You worried something was wrong with you physically. Then you did the natural thing and looked at your stool. Somehow, whatever you saw supported whatever you suspected: your bowel was sick and the consistency of your stool proved it. Actually, everyone's stool varies in consistency. It depends on a number of factors. There's your genetically determined way of absorbing food and liquids in the bowel and excreting them as waste. We all have different enzyme systems that accomplish this." I paused when I realized I was sounding like a physiology teacher.

"Additionally, we all eat different food and have different diets. The stool texture you observed was normal. What you did was jump to the conclusion that there was something wrong with you. And, quite naturally, you consulted a specialist. What has exacerbated your problem is that you won't accept your doctor's findings. Your symptoms were given the name irritable bowel syndrome. This name is not wrong, but it doesn't tell the whole story because this is a group of symptoms, not a diagnosis, and it can be associated with emotional discomfort and emotional disorders."

Arthur Walker listened raptly, hanging on to every detail of my "lecture." Surprised—and excited by his reaction, I continued my explanation, sensing I had his permission.

"Do you remember how you've mentioned that you burp a lot? All that burping you report—well, it's because you are swallowing air. This is common in people with heightened levels of anxiety. That air you swallow contributes to your stomach pains, the bloating, and gas."

He said nothing.

I went further, gently. "You know, you've never told me anything about your childhood. I am sure all sorts of things happened that encouraged you to lean toward physical rather than verbal expressions of your feelings. I can understand why, after all those rather traumatic psychiatric experiences, you have chosen to deemphasize the emotional. After all, having all these physical symptoms means you don't have to think of yourself as psychologically damaged.

"But this still doesn't fully explain why your mind chose this particular solution," I went on, "this particular way to avoid the painful past. Your mind could have chosen many other forms of expression. I am sure that some of the answers can be traced to your childhood—your parents' attitudes, perhaps. This is aside from the fact that physical symptoms such as yours are always part of something we call generalized anxiety disorder, and this is what I believe is your problem."

There! I finally used the term I had so studiously avoided. I now felt free to do so.

I went on in my best professional manner: "Like all emotional disorders, generalized anxiety disorder begins with an inborn vulnerability. In your case, it is a tendency to experience too much anxiety. You probably were also born with the tendency to use physical language to say that you are emotionally uncomfortable. The unique way in which you express these things is most likely determined by your upbringing."

As if a light had gone on, Walker reacted to the word *upbringing*. For the first time, he told me about his parents, his home life, and his school experiences. It seemed that failure was taboo in the Walker home. No one ever spoke about failure or even minor mistakes. Not that failure didn't exist. When his father, a paper manufacturer, suffered business reverses, no one spoke about them. The shame was too great to bear, let alone discuss, especially among family members.

The need to be perfect and the shame that should be felt when he wasn't were instilled in Arthur early on. "When I was nine, our schoolteacher passed out painting materials and told us to use our imagination and paint whatever we pleased. I can't remember what I painted, but I do remember being pleased by it—until the teacher held up my painting before the class, ridiculed it, and made my classmates laugh. I'll never forget that. I broke down in tears. I felt totally worthless."

He continued, "In my early teens, I was a fairly good athlete but never much of a distance runner. At an interschool track meet, I got beat in a race by a whole bunch of girls. No one ever heard of a boy being beat like that before. I wanted to hide. I couldn't face my family." He paused and then added, "These little failures are what count. Success counts for nothing."

With some insight, Walker then told me that in his home illness was equated with failure and thereby perceived as shameful. When his father, who I was now told was epileptic, fell and shattered his shoulder, his mother told everyone this was the result of a minor accident that happened while on a trip abroad. Walker's mother suffered from Parkinson's disease. Her shuffling was obvious to all, but her son was admonished never to ask her questions about her shuffling walk because she was very sensitive about it.

As a child, Walker was not sickly but had his share of childhood diseases—chicken pox, strep throat, flu. During those times, special attention was lavished on him, but no one ever spoke about what was wrong with him. Walker came to understand that this coded behavior meant that the greater and more tender the care and the less said about the illness, the more quickly this abhorrent circumstance would disappear.

It occurred to me that this was why his parents allowed him to be institutionalized and given shock treatment. Doing this removed both the ill person and the illness from their lives.

This complex mixture of emotional reaction to physical illness and feelings of embarrassment and shame was intensified and fixed by the events of his late adolescence—the "mental illness" and shock treatment. The increased care he received when ill as a child potentiated the expression of physical symptoms. At the same time, the shame of illness pushed the pendulum in the other direction, toward a denial of illness and an unacknowledged acceptance of anxiety. Only medical doctors could halt the pendulum's swing. Psychiatrists had been given a chance and found wanting. Later, just seeing them merely intensified his feelings of shame. He had come to see me for medication, and my ability to prescribe it made me more of a medical doctor than a psychiatrist. Paradoxically, he never missed a session and usually talked without interruption.

I now realized that, in a way, his wife resembled his parents. She cared deeply for him and was especially attentive during his (daily) bouts of anxiety and physical discomfort. Unlike his parents, however, she fed him a constant diet of medical information. She was an avid reader of medical literature and passed it on to her husband. She seemed to be as preoccupied with his illness as he was. She certainly never chided him or said anything like "Walker, get your act together." With her interest in medicine and her unusual tolerance for her husband's maladies, she was indeed an enabler, that is, someone who unconsciously wills the perpetuation of the somatic symptoms. In this sense, she was the "perfect wife."

I knew that Arthur Walker's symptoms of anxiety and his preoccupation with physical illness would never fully abate—chronic somatization symptoms rarely do—although their expression could be moderate and certainly tolerable. Yet, significantly, as he gained insight into his condition and came to see its emotional roots, the terms *hypoglycemia* and *irritable bowel syndrome* disappeared from both of our vocabularies. His symptoms now reappeared only under extremely stressful circumstances and, when they did, he reverted to moderating his diet in his accustomed manner. But even these symptoms and the frequency of their recurrence soon diminished.

I can even write a satisfying conclusion to Arthur Walker's story. After three years of never missing our monthly sessions, he called to tell me he had been recruited for a job on the West Coast, was flying to Seattle to work out the details, and would not be able to keep his next appointment. I congratulated him and offered to mail his prescription. Walker was not satisfied with this remedy for a missed session; he wanted an appointment for the following week. He wanted to see me and relate his good news personally. Things were now looking up for him, indeed. Not only had he been named a senior vice president and counsel to a Fortune 500 company, his wife was pregnant with their second child.

· 7 ·

The Princess, Her Husband, Her Lover, and Me

Once upon a time, there lived a beautiful Italian princess. All her wishes came true when she married a very wealthy man who wrapped her in furs and provided her with every luxury known to woman. She was not expected to ever lift a finger, only to be available to her "prince." Her every wish was anticipated by a devoted staff. She did not even have to leave her house, but, if she wanted to, a chauffeured limousine awaited. All was wonderful in fairyland until the princess developed a horrible malady that all the medical advisors in the land could not cure. Things were not going well in the realm of the mind of her royal highness. What follows is the tale of what happened when a psychiatrist was invited to enter that realm and how the princess's fairy-tale existence was changed.

The princess introduced herself abruptly: "I was in the middle of the street, Doctor. I couldn't walk. I couldn't get my breath. I was dizzy. My heart was racing a hundred miles an hour. I felt like I was choking. I thought I was going to die. I had to wait for the crowds to pass. I was nearly run over by all the cars. I don't go out anymore, Doctor. Not alone, because I'm too afraid. I only go out with my husband or my driver. Just to think about going out makes me nervous."

There was a mixture of desperation and timidity in her voice, giving her plight an urgency that demanded immediate attention and action. I was prepared to listen further. But instead of telling me more, she confronted me: "You don't know what it is, do you? Tell me, Doctor. You don't know what it is. Think about that, Doctor." The second *t* of *that* was hardened like a duplicated Italian consonant, giving it an almost hissing quality.

For a moment, I didn't know how to respond. Psychiatrists are trained to keep quiet at such times. But something about the forcefulness of her demands, the provocative quality of this very beautiful woman, and, perhaps, my own need to show how insightful I was made me blurt out, "You have panic disorder."

Although, technically, my response may have been premature, my diagnostic impression was quite valid. That I could arrive at a diagnosis after having heard so little says less for my professional acumen than it does for the specificity of the symptoms of panic disorder, which makes it among the easiest of disorders to diagnose, provided that a clear history of an episode can be elicited.

The princess ignored my assessment and continued talking. The tone of her voice rose like a musical scale. "It was on the escalator. I looked down, I saw the lines, the lines in the steps, I don't know. What do you call them? They are not straight. My eyes are playing tricks, Doctor. You know what's wrong with me? My husband was there, and I don't know what would have happened if he was not there. He took my arm and said very quietly, 'Don't worry, I'm with you, you will be OK.' He comforted me. *Sia lodato Gesù e Maria.* Thank God, he was there. He's so good, my husband. Too good. If he wasn't there, I don't know what I would do, maybe I faint. What's wrong with me?"

She stared at me directly but offered no chance for comment.

"It was hard for me to tell you this, Doctor. These are the most embarrassing moments of my life. I don't tell anyone. Maybe I did something wrong. Maybe I sinned. I don't think so, Doctor," she said, showing a gentler and more plaintive self.

If the princess made her emotional presence felt early and powerfully, her physical presence was equally as powerful. She was five feet nine inches tall and always wore high heels. The first time she came to my office, it was winter and she wore a full-length sable coat that made her appear soft yet regal. I recall how she carelessly slipped the fur coat off her shoulders with graceful feline gestures, exposing a lean, angular body in a simple, high-necked, long-sleeved black sweater dress. Her face was proportionately long, appearing just a little smaller than it really was because of her high cheekbones and somewhat sunken, large, almond-shaped, dark eyes. She might have been an inspiration for Modigliani.

Despite her bearing, I did not know she was a princess until her son called later and referred to her as such.

The princess revealed much more of her disorder that morning. "I've had this for fifteen years. I've been to see lots of doctors. My first attack happened fifteen years ago. At first, I thought it would go away, that it was just something that happened, God's will. Then, *Santa Maria*, it happened again. And again. Usually it was in the street. Once I was at a friend's house. It was a weird, how you say, weird feeling. It clicked in my head. I couldn't catch my breath. I fell from the sofa. My friend took me to the emergency room. They said there was nothing wrong with me. The doctors—those idiots—said there was nothing wrong with me, that all I needed was a rest. Of course, they say this. When I got to the emergency room, I was already feeling better, the attack was over. Seventeen times I went to the emergency room. Sometimes I would call the ambulance. They had to give me oxygen. Sometimes I felt like I had indigestion, a spasm. I thought I had a heart attack. I knew it would happen again. Of course, it did. Stupid doctors. After this, I stayed home. I was afraid to go out alone anymore. The funny thing is that when I go out with my husband or with my driver, I'm not afraid. I don't understand this."

She reverted to her commanding and, what I was coming to see, demanding self. She challenged me. "You must cure this, Doctor. There must be a cure. Dr. Fielding said he was sure you can help me. I come here because of him. There must be something to help me."

"There is," I said.

Again, she ignored me. I realized that she was not being condescending. Perhaps she had not heard me. I mused over an explanation for her obliviousness. She desperately wanted help for what she thought was a fallen state, but her inability to get it after fifteen years of seeking cures and solace had left her unprepared for offers of salvation. Nor, I supposed, did she feel that doctors could grant absolution. On the other hand, I thought, perhaps she heard me but just wanted to go on talking . . . get it all out . . . make her confession.

"I've got a noise in my heart, Doctor. I have an arrhythmia. The electrocardiogram shows it. My condition has something to do with my heart valve. Sometimes I hear it clicking. It happened once in the street when I heard it clicking and racing. The doctor put me on a medicine, Inderal, which made it better. My heart was slower and it didn't race as much. But it didn't stop the attacks, so I don't take it anymore. I threw it away."

She spoke rapidly. "I hate all doctors. I have so much medical wrong with me. I'm sure I have an ulcer. I worry so much, I feel depressed. But I won't take their pills. I don't take any vitamins. I don't go to doctors anymore. I saw too many. They said it was my thyroid. They said it was abnormal. They gave me medicine. They said this was the cause. It did nothing. I stopped taking it. Now they say my thyroid is fine. I wonder how this can be. But really, Doctor, my health is not good. I'm anemic because I don't eat right. This makes me weak. This is all caused by my health. Or, maybe I did something wrong. My husband thinks I'm mad to go to a psychiatrist."

Initially taken aback by her appearance, I was now struck by her preoccupation with illness. If I was right about panic disorder, then the symptoms she was describing could be part of the secondary hypochondria that accompanies it.

She went on, peppering her recitations with Italian phrases she seemed to assume I understood. "My husband. He's a wonderful man, Doctor. Anything I want, he gives to me. *Va bene.* He's the most generous man I know, kind and gentle. He likes me to be home. He likes it that I don't go out. He's an old-fashioned man, Doctor, and he wants me home. Not like the women today. *Santa Maria.* What kind of women are they, going to work every day, not caring for their husbands or children?"

She told me that her generous husband had also provided the chauffeur-driven limousine in which she traveled around the city and commuted to horse country on weekends. She said that for years she had not left her apartment unaccompanied.

"I think I know what is wrong with you." I was impatient to get to the heart of the matter and sensed that she had confessed enough for the moment. It was time to offer a gesture of absolution. I repeated, "You have an illness called panic disorder. There are medicines that can help you."

She quickly rejoined, "I'm not taking that depression medicine. They tried it on me. It made me sick."

I was sure I knew which medication she meant. It was probably Imipramine, an antidepressant drug, which in small doses is remarkably effective in controlling the symptoms of panic disorder. But, for a day or two, initially, it may worsen the symptoms, and, consequently, many patients often stop taking the drug almost as soon as they've started it. I didn't want to repeat this mistake with someone who had suffered so long. Instead, I used another approach and prescribed Xanax, a member of the benzodiazepine family of drugs and known to be effective in panic disorder (not all members of this family of drugs are). When the princess's immediate symptoms were ameliorated, I would add the antidepressant for long-term benefit.

"You're probably like all the others," she said. "You'll poison me." Then almost flippantly, and with an air of resignation, she raked her long fingers through her black hair and added, "I'll take the chance. Give it to me. But don't poison me. I'll try. *Va bene.*"

I took out my prescription pad, at the same time explaining that the treatment of panic disorder consisted not just of medication to take care of the panic attacks but also of seeing a psychiatrist to sort out the problems underlying and resulting from the illness. I advised weekly meetings. I do not think she heard much of my discourse, but she consented to follow my advice nevertheless.

"*Va bene,*" she said. "I'll see you next week."

It had all been too easy—my rapid diagnosis and offer of treatment, her acceptance after seeming early reluctance. I felt proud of my rapid diagnosis and the prospect of helping a woman others could not. I did not contemplate how removing her symptoms might affect her and her family, change her whole fairy-tale existence, and force her to find new but incomplete solutions to her altered circumstances. Nor did I expect that I would later come to question if my treatment had been correct.

Panic disorder, which I felt was at the heart of the princess's problem, is a serious illness. Thirteen million Americans have it, 70 percent of them women. In panic disorder, the anxiety is present only when the attack occurs. Thoughts or actions don't cause the attacks; they occur because of a change in body chemistry. When the attack occurs—it can last for ten minutes or more— people experience rapid heart rate, rapid breathing, and dizziness. They think they are going to die or maybe go crazy. The place where they have their first attack becomes the place they are most afraid to go back to, because they think they are going to get another attack if they do. After a few attacks, they may anticipate another attack by not going out at all. So they stay home. Some people feel so bad that they try to commit suicide.

By the time people with panic disorder see a doctor, the attack has passed. The doctor commonly attributes the incident to "nerves" and may prescribe tranquilizers that do nothing to help. When this doesn't work, the doctor may undertake an extensive medical workup. The tests show nothing, but people with panic disorder persist and consult many doctors. Searching for explanations, they ascribe the attacks to other causes, for example, to something in their past that they are ashamed of. If they are religious, they may think that the attacks are punishment for their wrongdoings. They stop telling friends and family about their situation.

People with panic disorder often have a heart murmur, the result of a condition called mitral valve prolapse, in which one of the heart valves sinks in its cylindrical container. This, in itself, is not serious. But when the heart murmur is heard, it confirms the sufferer's fears that something physical is wrong. In addition to the effects of the presence of the murmur and whatever physical symptoms accompany the attacks, people with panic disorder are hypochondriacal—secondary hypochondria—all the time. Once the panic disorder is diagnosed and treated, the somatization symptoms lessen.

The princess returned to her next session feeling much better. The anticipatory anxiety was reduced. It would still be some weeks before she ventured even the shortest distance out of her Park Avenue aerie alone. When she did, it was a triumph akin to a child taking her first steps. Not one to minimize her achievements (or failures), the princess likened her newfound freedom to flying. "I love to fly, Doctor. Since I'm a child, I love to fly. Then I feel I have wings."

For a few months, the princess and I were content with her progress. Her mood soared. I was pleased that I had helped someone so crippled, so beautiful.

The only discordant notes struck during this period were her continuing reports of physical symptoms that I viewed as hypochondriacal. She believed that the glands in her neck were enlarged. She left Dr. Fielding and, through friends, found a new internist who proceeded to order a battery of tests and repeat many investigations, including a CAT scan of her brain. She underwent these tests but rejected their negative feelings. I felt that she exaggerated her doctor's assessment of her medical condition. She dramatized everything in her life. When I invited her thoughts about these symptoms, she said that her father had died of an illness with enlarged nodes in his neck.

The next major episode involving the princess occurred about three months after our first meeting and took me by surprise.

"That man—my husband . . . ," she began. "He made me stay at home and imprisoned me. Now I see it all. He was happy that I was sick so I would stay home and be only his. He did not have to share me with anyone else. I had to give up all my friends. Wherever I went, I went with the driver. I needed him, the driver. But now I don't need him anymore. I'm free. Now I see how he needed for me to be imprisoned, like in a cage. Of course, he was generous. He had his little girl at home, his to play with. I never said no to him. Every night, he wanted me. Never enough. *Madonna*. I tried. It was not always easy, but I never said no."

She crossed herself.

What she was telling me was that her husband, a wealthy industrialist, had enabled her symptoms all these years. If he considered her condition at all, he thought that he had a very "neurotic" wife. He had not prevented her from consulting many physicians, and if they were unable to change her symptoms, how could he be expected to do so? As long as she fulfilled his needs, he had no need to conceive of her symptoms differently or change the circumstances of their lives.

I had not yet perceived the extent of the changes taking place in the princess's household. Although I asked her to ask her husband to see me, he refused. I had to depend on her for descriptions. She said he was fifty, shorter than she, immaculately dressed, and unfailingly courteous. I was reminded of a story by Alberto Moravia in which a nattily dressed, kind, and generous travel agent is tortured by his neurotic, housebound, beautiful wife who keeps threatening to throw herself from the window. He, like the princess's husband, was indulgent to a fault, abetting her behavior.

At our sessions, the princess showed her seductive side, deliberately angling her body to emphasize her breasts and allowing her skirt to settle high on her slender thighs. The scent of her perfume clung to the upholstery for many sessions after hers. With a sultry air, she would frequently say, "It's you that has freed me, Doctor. You have made me fly. I love you for this. *Va bene.*"

I cannot deny that she affected me and aroused admittedly unpsychiatric feelings. Her husband was her "prince," while I was the commoner freeing the beautiful princess in danger, using Xanax, my powerful sword.

One day, after I had been seeing the princess for a year, she told me that her daughter, who was fourteen and lived at home, was about to take a trip alone to Europe.

"How do you feel about her going off alone?" I asked.

"I have a special connection with my daughter. She doesn't need to write to us. I know what she is thinking."

Sensing that this might be a recapitulation of her relationship with her own mother, I asked about their relationship.

"My mother? She's still in the old country, in Sicily. Now she lives all the time on the estate, high up in the mountains. When I was a child, we used to live in the city part of the year. The other part, we went up to the estate. No one cared if I went to school. I refused anyway. I preferred staying home with my mother."

It was not difficult for me to believe that this willful woman could have refused to go to school and gotten away with it.

She continued. "There were a few estates, but we stayed always in my favorite. It had been renovated and was in better shape than the others. They were all from the eighteenth century. I miss it so much, I go back often. We had to take a train up to the estate. That was my favorite trip. We went in a train without corridors, without a toilet. Mama brought a chamber pot with her for the children to use, and we used to throw the you-know-what out the window."

She smiled nostalgically and went on, "My father loved me. He played games with me. He told me I was his favorite little girl, his beautiful princess. I loved him, too. He always took such good care of me. I *was* his little girl."

She looked sadder. I had grown used to her rapidly changing moods.

"*Mio caro padre* died when I was fifteen and Mama went into mourning. I think she was sad for a long time. She stayed inside the house for three years. I had to stay with her. My brothers and sisters took care of business affairs.

"I knew my father was going to die. A little before he died, everyone made a toast to him. Everybody said, '*Molti anni*'— 'Many years,' that was our traditional toast. I said, '*Per poco*'— 'For a short while!' My father heard this; so did everyone else. Later, when I said I knew my father was going to die, everybody said I was psychic. It's true, Doctor. I can tell what is going to happen. I always knew that one day I would find you, and you would help me."

I had noticed that the princess always wore black. I asked her whether her mother wore black after her father died.

"Of course, she wore black after this. She always wore black. That's what we did in the old country."

"Is that why you always wear black?"

She became hostile, as she usually did when I asked pointed questions. When she got angry, she gave the impression of almost leaping out of the chair with her body elongated, like a leopard in flight.

"Black suits me. That's why I wear it. It looks good on me," she hissed.

I could not disagree.

"Anyway, Doctor, black is the color of melancholy, of depression. I have always felt this way." She smiled again.

I ventured an interpretation. "I think that when your father died, your life stood still, like your mother's. You are so connected to your mother that you replicated what she did. The two of you have continued to mourn for your father. You never really gave him up, accepted that he was dead. Like your mother, you remain in mourning to this day and show it by wearing black."

She didn't respond but seemed engrossed by what I was saying. I went on, "Your husband has substituted for your father. This kind and generous man keeps you like a little girl, his little princess. And you are connected to your daughter, just as you are to your mother. That's why you think you know what she's thinking. Your mind and hers are one."

"I don't believe it!"

We did not return to this subject for a long time. But this conversation stimulated my thinking about an important factor in panic disorder patients. They have had great difficulty separating from their mothers (long before the onset of their panic attacks). Some researchers have also noticed a high incidence of childhood separation anxiety disorder, usually school phobia, in these patients.

This would explain the princess's "refusal" to go to school as a youngster. It was not her willfulness that kept her home, as she would have me believe. Instead, the prospect of leaving her mother terrified her. It also crystallized for me how the princess's willfulness often concealed her underlying terror.

How separation fears are related to panic disorder is not clear. It is theorized that difficulties in development occur in the latter part of the first year of life when separation from the mother is first attempted. These may be a part of the genetic vulnerability to panic disorder. It is not by accident that panic disorder patients become agoraphobic, staying home and totally avoiding public places, as the princess did. Her particular life circumstances and traumas determined the specifics of the expression of her fears of separation. In the princess's case, her father's death was pivotal in further cementing her bonds with her mother. This event also provided a subterfuge to disguise the real meaning of her inability to leave her mother and go to school. Similarly, this event influenced her later choice of a marriage partner, who, like her father, adored her and encouraged her to be housebound and dependent, and enabled her to hide the true nature of her problems.

Given her newfound freedom, the princess was unhappy that she had not been able to find a constructive and productive niche for herself. In a sense, her panic disorder had been protective of her inability to accomplish in the past; she could hide behind the cloak of illness.

Sometimes she said, "I feel I'm no good, there's nothing I can do. I'm useless."

At other times, she said, "Do you think I'm stupid? I'm smart, Doctor. Just because I'm not working doesn't mean I'm not smart."

I avoided talking about any subject that might reflect on her intellect, because when I did, she would spend the next ten minutes justifying her intelligence to me.

Now able to go out alone, the princess was taking many trips, not only to Italy but all over the world. She always sent me postcards with the same message: "I miss our talks."

Between trips, she resumed treatment and spoke mainly about how free she felt. I noted that she made a concerted effort to wear clothes of different colors. Clearly, this was to please me. She liked black; it was her, it was her past, it was hard to relinquish.

Despite this reluctance to divest herself of the symbols of her past, her present life was changing. She dropped hints about all the men, young and old, who wanted to seduce her, but she never elaborated. She teased me in this way. I realized that she was now "free" in more than one sense of the word.

"Do you have lovers?" I asked one day.

She exploded. "How dare you suggest this? I am—you know I am—faithful to my husband. He is such a kind and generous man. I would never do this to him. I love him."

I knew that the princess was not above lying, but I reserved judgment and returned to thinking about her secondary hypochondria when she began a discussion of her symptoms. According to the textbooks, they should have disappeared, but they never completely did. She continued to see her doctors, now consulting physicians all over Europe as well as the United States. As always, she explained all her medical symptoms and stressed that the doctors thought they were serious. And, as always, she rejected their advice.

One trip lasted longer than the others. When she returned, she was glowing. "I've met him. He's so wonderful, tall and handsome, spiritually and physically. A widower. His wife died last year. He's German, and he lives in Hamburg. I'm going to leave my husband, move in with Alfred. He wants this." After a pause, she added, "My husband swallowed me. He still wants me all the time. I can't respond to him."

I started to feel concerned. In my old-fashioned way, I do not like to see family ties imperiled. And I began to realize that alleviating the princess's symptoms did more than allow her to leave her gilded cage. The ramifications of the patient's successful treatment were now evident, and I felt guilty. It was silly for me to think this way. I had an obligation to help her and had done so. Now that she was better, she had a perfect right to live with whomever she wanted to.

Soon after this discussion, the princess left on one of her extended vacations. She wrote me a long letter indicating that her fairy-tale existence had been shaken. She was torn between her past and the new order of her life. One does not simply change fifteen years of panic attacks and their consequences without a long period of adjustment. The new order of her life was certainly freer and healthier, but it brought fresh problems. She needed to maintain her family ties, both emotionally and morally. They represented a necessary continuation of her deep attachment to her past, her childhood, and its traumas. She was torn between this and her need to live a euphoric, freer life with a liberating man. She opted for a middle road, a partial solution: retain her family and her husband, have a lover, and maintain her contact with me.

There was another troubling aspect to her newfound conflicts. The panic disorder had protected her from ever having to do more than stay home. Now she had no such ready excuse and it tugged at her, making her feel newly inadequate. She seemed to be avoiding these feelings by traveling all over the world and reinforcing her shaken self-esteem by acting on her seductive impulses.

The princess continued traveling extensively and returned to

New York to her other specialists and me every few months. She continued to have vague medical complaints for which her doctors could find no medical reason. From time to time, the princess called me from Paris, Rome, Milan, Hamburg, or Sicily. She appeared to go to her ancestral home regularly. She would always tell me how free she felt and how much I had helped her before switching the conversation to her latest plans for redecorating the castle. Whenever these calls came, I would reflect on my experience of treating the princess. I suppose I could have pondered the effectiveness of medication in panic disorder or thought about how doctors still relegate panic disorder to the realm of the hysterical. I could have thought about the many weighty issues this disorder raises. I did, but other thoughts pressed on my mind. I had liberated the princess from her panic attacks, but my psychiatric treatment did not guarantee her happiness. There is life after psychiatric treatment. *Va bene.*

·8·

The Case of the
Misleading Symptoms

In the early years of my psychiatric training, I presented a difficult patient to a teacher esteemed for both her clinical skills and worldly wisdom. I was worried about what would happen if the treatment plan I was pursuing didn't work out and the results were poor. She admonished me by reminding me that I was dealing with a human being and no matter how careful I was, I could not know in advance how any case would turn out. She reminded me that some of the most difficult beginnings have the most favorable endings and added that the reverse was sometimes also true.

At the time, I was unable to fully appreciate the implications of her words, but, over the years, I have come to cherish their wisdom. I still find the route from difficult beginning to favorable ending tortuous and exhausting, especially when the patient has numerous diagnoses, both psychological and physical, layered one on top of the other.

William Wallace was such a patient. I knew at our first meeting that his would be a complex diagnostic and treatment problem, but I never anticipated the extent of the challenge. I treated him over a four-year period, sometimes regularly, sometimes intermittently, and at all times he taxed my full intellect and every emotion. I spent most of the time diagnosing all his ills. As each diagnosis unfolded, the ensuing treatment brought new challenges, problems, and frustrations. But I think Bill and I would agree that the effort was worth it.

Bill was twenty-one when I first met him and had just graduated from college in Washington, D.C. The grayness of his skin made him appear much older. His face was round and moon shaped, his eyes were dull, and his body seemed limp, although he was quite muscular. I noticed that his ankles were swollen. His shirt and jeans were washed out, and I equated their appearance with his. His speech also had a lackluster, monotonous quality, making it difficult to listen to him.

Bill said that he had come to see me because he feared going to work. He said that he would get sick if he did. His fears were not without reason. Since childhood he had been both physically and mentally ill. He said that when he was fifteen, he developed ulcerative colitis, a chronic, debilitating, and often deadly disease of the lower bowel, the symptoms of which are bloody diarrhea and acute abdominal cramps. It carries the possibility of complications that are equally as life threatening: dilation and perforation of the bowel, anemia, and cancer. Sufferers plan their lives around the availability of bathrooms, because their need for them is so great. They have the pasty, sickly appearance that Bill had.

Many physicians believe that psychological factors contribute to ulcerative colitis and that individuals with particular personality types are apt to be more prone than others to this illness. Thus ulcerative colitis is thought to be psychosomatic, an *identifiable physical illness* whose origins include emotional factors. This condition is quite different from hypochondria, where, as we know, no evidence of physical disease can be uncovered.

For the treatment of his ulcerative colitis, Bill's doctors prescribed the cortisone-based drug Prednisone. He had tried many other drugs; none was successful. However, taking Prednisone for any length of time swells the body and face, raises the blood sugar, depletes the bones, and changes the body metabolism. At high-dosage levels, Prednisone can induce severe emotional changes, including psychosis, a major mental disorder in which the ability to interpret reality is grossly impaired.

At regular dosage levels, it produces an elevated mood, which can decline suddenly when the medication is withdrawn or the dose lowered. Bill's doses of Prednisone fluctuated from sixty to twenty-five milligrams, depending on the severity of the bloody diarrhea and spasms. When the dose was lowered to below twenty-five milligrams, he became depressed and jittery. Therefore, he refused to take less than that and, in this sense, he had become "hooked" on the steroid. Throughout the years I saw Bill, I continually urged him to take the smallest dose possible, because of the side effects. He did not listen to me until very late in the treatment.

Shortly after the onset of his ulcerative colitis, Bill developed an emotional illness, obsessive compulsive disorder. Obsessions are recurrent and persistent ideas, impulses, or images that are experienced as intrusive and senseless. Compulsions, in contrast, are behaviors that are repetitive, purposeful, and intentional. They are performed according to certain rules or in a stereotyped fashion (rituals) and are designed to prevent some dreaded event or situation. Some of these features are present in many people, but to a limited degree. Therefore to be diagnosed as a *disorder,* the obsessions or compulsions must cause marked distress, be time-consuming, and significantly interfere with a person's normal occupational or social functioning.

Bill's was a classic case of obsessive compulsive disorder, and he was aware that it was interfering with his life. He dreaded germs. In response to this fear, he initiated a series of behaviors designed to "disinfect" himself. He washed his face and hands at least thirty times a day, performing these ablutions ritually, until they occupied hours of his time. If he saw people in the street touch their stomachs, Bill assumed that they had intestinal flu and would infect him. He literally ran from them as fast as he could, headed for the first men's room, and washed himself with hospital-strength soap that he carried in his backpack. Similarly, he avoided nose blowers or even people with handkerchiefs sticking out of their pockets. He searched the sidewalks for hints of contamination by dirty water, oil, or refuse. He feared rabies and cringed when he saw a dead animal.

From the start of our relationship, he was preoccupied with AIDS. In his mind, it was universal and easily caught. Every man he encountered was carefully scrutinized for evidence of homosexuality: being too well dressed, having a high-pitched voice, making a less-than-masculine gesture, or giving a furtive look— all were indicative of a homosexual male who was to be avoided. He established similar criteria for drug addicts. No reassurance or logical argument could change his beliefs.

He confessed he was depressed and wanted treatment because he knew that these thoughts and actions were not normal. He blamed his behavior on masturbation, an activity that he said gave him pleasure but filled him with guilt.

Listening to him, I considered whether a depressive disorder might have increased or worsened his symptoms. Diagnosing depressive disorder in the physically ill is always hard because the symptoms of depressive disorder and physical illness often overlap. Sick individuals feel low, eat poorly, lose weight, and have disturbed sleep and diminished functioning—all features of depressive disorder. But most very ill people do not have the feelings of extreme hopelessness and despair of those with depressive disorder. In Bill's case, making an accurate diagnosis was complicated by the presence of Prednisone, which precipitated depressed feelings.

I asked Bill whether he was eating and sleeping well. He answered that he was sleeping well. His appetite was okay, too. I asked him to tell me about his thoughts. They were neither extremely gloomy nor hopeless, and I put a diagnosis of depressive disorder aside.

I asked him about his family. He said he lived with his mother, father, and two sisters. Bill was close to his mother; his father traveled and was hardly visible. One sister, with whom he got along well, was about to enter college and another had recently married and had moved to Denver.

Over the course of the next few sessions, Bill gave me a fuller history of his psychological and physical problems. Interestingly, in compulsive style, he presented his story chronologically, remembering where he had left off previously. He balanced each set of physical problems with a corresponding set of emotional ones, sometimes changing the order of the category presented first. The effect gave a certain rhythm, organization, and symmetry to his presentation.

When he was seven, an aunt died of a heart attack. When his mother heard the news, she slipped on the kitchen floor and broke her arm. Bill blamed himself for his mother's accident. At eight, Bill was admitted to the hospital with pneumonia and then spent several weeks at home recovering. He remembered not wanting to go to school because he was certain something would happen to his mother while he was away. Even when he was healthy again, he was absent a lot and his teacher sent him to the school psychologist. Bill said he liked talking with her.

At nine he had a sore throat all the time and was always on antibiotics. He was often constipated, and his mother regularly gave him laxatives and enemas. His schoolwork was poor, and he switched schools but still called the psychologist to talk to her. The sore throats continued until he was twelve. His relationship with the psychologist faded. He developed a love of sugar. He ate candy all day long and added sugar to all his foods.

At fifteen, he started having hives and rashes and was tested for allergies, but none could be found. At the same time, he said he made a pact with his mother. He would give up candy if she would buy him the stereo equipment he wanted. He also started to exercise and became an avid hockey player. Soon after, he developed the first symptoms of ulcerative colitis, although it took doctors almost a year until they made a definitive diagnosis. He said that was when he really started to worry about his health. He thought his illness came from giving up sugar and started eating candy again.

As the symptoms of ulcerative colitis continued, he started to have nightly anxiety attacks, fearing he would die if he fell asleep. He was referred to a psychiatrist. The next few years, until I saw him, were marked by never-ending visits to doctors. His mother heard about hypoglycemia on a radio talk show. She insisted he see several hypoglycemia experts, having decided that his ulcerative colitis came from eating candy. The experts concurred with her "diagnosis" and put Bill on a strict diet that measured his sugar intake. He also took megadoses of vitamins as his fears of illness magnified.

By the time he was eighteen, Bill was a veteran patient. He had endured pain, had been subjected to innumerable tests and treatments, and had become well versed in medical terms and procedures. At this point, Prednisone therapy was introduced, his colitis symptoms subsided, and for the first time in years he felt "healthy." Bill's newfound health did not preclude his preoccupation with germs, however. Now in college, he spent most of his free time bathing and cleaning his room.

At this time when he was better physically, his physicians attempted to reduce the Prednisone. As they did, physical symptoms returned. He said that he sweated profusely and his "bones felt cold." But the emotional response to the drop in dosage troubled him more. He reported daily mood swings. Different tranquilizers were tried, all with limited success. Despite his physical weakness and mood swings, he played varsity hockey, practiced daily, and forced himself to endure full games, putting all his energy into the sport.

Listening to Bill over those first weeks of his treatment, I heard the detailed history of a man whose young life had been shaped by physical illness and emotional problems. He had a long history of consulting physicians and a profound knowledge of the medical aspects of his case and his medications. Many aspects of his childhood history needed to be weighed.

There was more than a hint of hypochondriasis dating back to early childhood. He was a professional patient, totally absorbed in himself, with little regard for others, who were there only to service his needs. He and his mother had subjected him to the many and various theories that hypochondriacs seek out to explain their symptoms. Theirs was a world of concern with sugar intake, vitamin deficiencies, and allergies. I had every reason to believe what Bill was telling me, particularly because his story seemed to mesh with the information I had gotten from the internist who referred him. Later on in the treatment, he would introduce new, conflicting information—but, for the moment, I had to rely on what I had been told. Frankly, with the material I had, I did not know how to approach Bill's case. This was before drugs for obsessive compulsive disorder were available, and I decided to continue treating him with psychotherapy.

I made this decision because he had seen other psychiatrists periodically and found them helpful. Moreover, he had come to me voluntarily, and I reasoned that he regarded psychiatrists as beneficial in some way; but I would have to wait to discover why. He accepted my recommendation and agreed to continue our meetings.

He spoke about his life and his compulsions. He challenged me to refute the logic of his fears and rituals. "If I inadvertently touch the sleeve of a fag, will I get AIDS? If I stand near someone who is coughing, will I get TB? If I see a well-dressed man in the bus, does that mean he's homosexual? If I see a stray dog, will it have rabies? If I see white powder in the street, is it lime and will it blind me?"

If I was reluctant to answer, he would nag, repeating the question again and again. He was compelled both to think and oppose his illogical thoughts. The struggle inside him was wearying, and he wearied me, too, as I futilely tried to relieve the tension and placate him by pointing out the illogicality of his thoughts.

"Do you think it will make a difference if I understand that what I'm thinking is illogical?" he asked.

"How will it do that?" I asked.

"Somehow, I just think that if I keep saying to myself that this is all crazy, not real, I'll feel better. And it helps me if you say so as well."

I now understood one of the reasons Bill wanted to see a psychiatrist. I realized he expected a psychiatrist would have mystical curative powers that would protect him from all his fears. He wanted to borrow my curative powers to overcome his warped thinking. Obsessive compulsive people often believe in magic.

I found it heartbreaking to watch him exhaust himself when he was already so frail, and I did not know how to change this. All I had to offer was supportive psychotherapy. If he felt that coming to see me helped, then I supposed we should continue our meetings. I felt my approach was somewhat vindicated when, almost a year later, Bill announced he had found a job. He was jubilant. I had never seen him in better mood.

"I'll be working at Macy's. They're starting me out at the bottom, with inventory mainly. But I know I'm going to rise to the top pretty soon. I've been thinking I'll be the chairman of this company. I know I will."

Bill was doing better than I had ever imagined he would. At the same time that he was enthusiastically starting up the corporate ladder, he was sending signals that something more than just obsessive compulsive disorder was brewing. I wondered about his exaggerated sense of accomplishment and I made the following note: "I wonder what lurks under his compulsive symptomatology?" But I left the thought on paper.

Because he had not increased his dose of Prednisone, his elation was not related to this drug. I was too taken with Bill's progress to recognize his high spirits and enthusiasm as anything but appropriate in a young man just starting out. Indeed, when he spoke about leaving home, I was caught off guard. So soon? What progress! But I had my concerns, too. Patients with ulcerative colitis often associate the onset of their first symptoms with leaving home and separating from their mothers. Bill had told me that as a child he had difficulty separating from his mother.

I recognized an opportunity to work on a specific task: his fears of separation. I urged him to talk about his mother, hoping that he would reveal the thoughts and fantasies surrounding his attachment to her. Instead, however, he exploded with rage. This was not the first time he had done so. It seemed that every time I now spoke about his mother and leaving home, he became more and more irritable. I attributed his anger and irritability to his style of avoiding these painful subjects, a common reaction. I became even more concerned about his leaving home.

In retrospect, I realized I had made a mistake. In only pursuing an understanding of the psychological roots of his mood change, I neglected to consider fully the diagnostic implication of his inflated ambitions, his irritability, and his angry outbursts which were all part of his mood change. These represented a major turnaround for this sickly young man who was normally docile and mournful. My understandings were not wrong, but by limiting myself to psychological understanding alone, I undermined the search for accurate diagnosis and inadvertently subverted his treatment.

What followed, however, was more the result of Bill's mood change than my failure to comprehend the diagnostic implications of his altered mood state. He abruptly moved out of his parents' home and into an apartment with a girl he had dated at college. He announced that he was leaving treatment, telling me that the help he sought was too slow in coming. In passing, he said that his ulcerative colitis symptoms had flared up.

I needed time to analyze what had transpired. I had not given enough thought to the idea that his past and present mood swings were part of a mood disorder we call "mania." The situation *was* complicated. Prednisone *can* cause mood changes and I *had* thought of mania, although I had excluded it as a cause. Moreover, the points of his history that I failed to consider were indeed quite subtle and could have been missed by anyone.

As I reconsidered them with the benefit of hindsight, the relevant points of Bill's history became clearer. For example, his feverish athletic activity at college while under siege of serious physical illness, whatever the cause, represented more than a need to overcome weakness and appear macho. It is extremely difficult for a young man as sick and debilitated as Bill to pursue strenuous athletic activities. But people whose moods are elevated by their manic illness often have the capacity to exert themselves as Bill did. I remembered treating a young student who ran the Boston marathon without ever having previously run, exercised, or even trained; but then I had quickly recognized her manic symptoms.

Bill called me a year later and said he wanted to come back into treatment. His mood had reverted to its usual, somewhat sober state. Since I had seen him, he had left the job at Macy's because, he said, his ulcerative colitis had flared up again, moved back to his parents' house, and been hospitalized.

"I blame myself for having gotten sick again," he started. "I know I got sick because things were looking up. Whenever I am successful, I make things go wrong. I get sick again. I want to fail. That's the story of my life."

Here we were again, with the physical and the psychological balancing each other. But this time I had a deeper insight. Balancing oppositional forces is a trademark of obsessive personalities. For example, rituals of cleansing are designed to purge evil germs. This quirk of mind also explained why Bill presented his history with such symmetry. He felt that one group of conditions neutralized the other. Did this mean he would never be free of illness? I realized the implications of my thinking.

Blaming himself was now a prominent theme. I recognized that there was another side to his preoccupation with blame. If he were able to *make* himself sick, by whatever inexplicable means, he could assume some control of his life.

"I sometimes feel like getting into my mother's bed," he said. "When I'm ill, I feel very close to her. It makes no difference whether I'm physically or psychologically ill."

I had thought his belief that his medical illness would protect him from emotional illness, and vice versa, had serious implications. Being both psychologically and physically ill kept him close to his mother. As long as he maintained a symbiotic attachment to her, he would not get well. I also suspected that his mother was encouraging his behavior at some level, because it was equally as important for her to remain one with him.

Bill confirmed my suspicions. "I'm embarrassed to tell you this. I actually do get into my mother's bed at night and sleep next to her. I try to sleep on my own, but I'm too nervous because I think I'm going to die. Then I start to think my mom is going to die. I have to go to her, stay with her."

The fears that he and his mother were going to die confirmed the extent of their symbiotic attachment.

Bill saw me sporadically over the next two and one half years. He did not go to work and lived at home while his parents supported him. I learned that he and his father hardly spoke to each other. In fact, Bill said his father was not concerned that his only son stayed home. Bill was sufficiently insightful to recognize that his father encouraged the unconscious need of mother and son to be one. Bill's illness helped the family rationalize this situation. After all, you wouldn't expect a sick person to work or support himself.

Indeed, Bill was sick. Still taking Prednisone, he now developed a new symptom, incontinence. I pushed for more details here, but he remained somewhat vague and unresponsive. I interpreted this to mean that he was embarrassed by this latest turn and, perhaps, wanted to spare me the dirty details. I assumed that his incontinence was related to his ulcerative colitis.

My acceptance that he had only a single bowel disorder led me to dismiss this new symptom too perfunctorily. I failed to give enough weight to his description of his stool as hard and pebbly rather than loose, mucousy, or bloody, as it is in ulcerative colitis. I also failed to pay sufficient attention to other things that Bill told me: he was not incontinent at home, and he was only apprehensive about being so before he left the house.

Bill did leave home in the evenings. He saw his girlfriend every night. She knew about his incontinence and accepted it. They had a sexual relationship, mostly masturbatory, because their religion forbade premarital intercourse. I found this somewhat curious because he had once blamed his obsessive compulsive disorder on masturbation. Nonetheless, he was obviously not inhibited in this area, which I interpreted as a positive sign. On the other hand, I suspected that his inhibitions about intercourse were not just religiously determined. He confirmed my assumption that his perception, like that of other obsessives, of women's genitals as dirty was the cause of this.

Often Bill made an appointment, did not keep it, and did not call to cancel. Sometimes I did not hear from him for weeks. After one of these sabbaticals, he returned with serious depressive symptoms that he said started when his sister got married. He looked grayer and even more washed-out than usual. As I had come to anticipate, his bowel condition was controlled; in fact, he was now constipated.

The symptoms of depressive disorder frequently sound physical rather than emotional, and Bill spoke mainly of physical concerns. He had lost twenty-three pounds, seven in the previous week alone. He had no appetite. Such rapid weight loss is seen in depressive disorder and was particularly pertinent here because there was no physical reason to account for it. He also had thoughts of killing himself.

Bill continued, "I had a kidney stone about two months ago. Ever since then, I've been drinking loads of water. Some days I drink a gallon or more. I started to feel depressed. I increased the Prednisone on my own to thirty-two and a half milligrams. I know my body craves cortisone, and I feel I should take even more. I thought this would help my depression, but it hasn't this time."

He paused to lick his dry lips. "I worry more about AIDS. I know I really have it. My kidney stone was no accident. There is something wrong with my kidneys, and AIDS is the cause. I probably have TB and MS as well. AIDS definitely. My kidneys are dehydrating me and cleaning my blood and taking more fluid out and leading to dehydration."

I was struck by the sudden lapse of medical expertise in one usually so fluent and well versed in these matters. His description of kidney symptoms and AIDS made no sense physiologically. Yet he was convinced of the presence of the illness as he described it, and no amount of logic could dissuade him. This view of illness represented a change from his previous attitudes. He was no longer just worried about medical conditions; he now accepted his concerns as completely rational and normal. He was delusional.

Delusions are firm, fixed beliefs that go counter to all prevailing societal norms. When they involve body parts, they are called somatic delusions. Delusions are usually bizarre and easily recognized by others as aberrational. Somatic delusions, however, may go unrecognized because the patient apprehensively conceals them, the doctor does not sufficiently pursue details in the person's history, or the observer is unschooled in anatomy and physiology.

The delusional person acts on his convictions. Those with somatic delusions either pursue medical investigation ferociously or steadfastly refuse to see a doctor. No amount of medical investigation can contradict the belief that serious illness exists, and the doctor conveying reports of negative findings is perceived as too afraid to tell the truth or as maliciously hiding it. In extreme cases where the patient believes his death is imminent—for example, if he feels he has end-stage cancer—no amount of reassurance and urging will convince him to see any doctor or accept any treatment. Somatic delusions can be part of the clinical picture of depressive disorder.

Indeed, Bill was showing signs of depressive disorder: loss of sexual libido and strong guilt feelings. He had stopped having any sexual contact with his girlfriend; he had no desire. He felt guilty about having had sex with her and saw his current physical illness as a just punishment for his previous indulgence in premarital sex. He said, "If I cut out all pleasures, maybe I'll get better. I'll try hard to lead a clean life."

Bill also had the hopeless feelings that accompany depressive disorder. He was sure he was going to die. He contemplated suicide. He related these feelings to his mortal illness, rather than to depression. Because of his strong suicidal thoughts, I decided to hospitalize him.

Bill responded well to treatment of his depressive disorder in the controlled circumstances of the hospital, where his gastroenterologist was available to check his physical symptoms and his dosages of medication could be carefully monitored. I prescribed the antidepressant Imipramine and the major tranquilizer Navane, an accepted combination of medications for delusional depression. The gastroenterologist was able to reduce Bill's Prednisone dose to twenty-five milligrams again. Within two weeks, Bill started to feel wonderful, even a little high in mood. His "AIDS-related kidney ailment" disappeared. He gained weight. I was pleased and, with the concurrence of his gastroenterologist, I discharged him from the hospital.

At his first office visit following his hospitalization, Bill was full of questions about his medication. Although he knew all about ulcerative colitis medications, psychotropic drugs were new to him. If I explained all their side effects, he might not take them or he might manipulate the dose, as he had done with Prednisone. Nonetheless, I had an obligation to inform him.

Among the most serious side effects of Imipramine were lowered blood pressure and difficulty passing urine (the latter of particular concern given his history of kidney stones). Navane can cause a particularly alarming side effect where the neck twists, the tongue thickens, and the eyes roll. In addition, Navane can be responsible for the irreversible side effect tardive dyskinesia, characterized by persistent mouth, tongue, or limb movement. Bill was alarmed when I shared this information, as I expected him to be.

At home, Bill consulted his personal library of medical texts to gain a fuller appreciation of the effects of the drugs. The following week, he came to his session complaining that his legs were shaking. I didn't see this. But he saw this as evidence of tardive dyskinesia, although he had read that this side effect usually takes six months to develop. On his own, he decided to discontinue the Navane.

I wondered what to do. Bill needed these medications, because the chances of relapse of depression were high without them. Then I had an idea. I would use a medication similar to Navane but less likely to produce tardive dyskinesia. This medication, Thorazine, might have an additional benefit. While controlling his delusional thinking, it could also exert a direct inhibiting effect on the bowel, reducing resurgent diarrhea and incontinence. I shared this information with him.

Bill accepted this medication and, not long after, took off once more, as he had done so many times before. I did not see him until a year later. During the year he was away, he lived in Philadelphia, where he attended graduate school and lived with his girlfriend. He saw a psychiatrist, who prescribed the newly introduced drug Clomipramine for his obsessive compulsive disorder. This drug was available only from Canada, because the Food and Drug Administration had not yet approved its use in this country. (It was mailed to him.) When Bill was overwhelmed by its side effects, he stopped taking it.

This time when Bill returned, I prescribed Prozac, at that time a new drug said to be equally effective in depression and obsessive compulsive disorder. As I carefully observed him, I gradually increased the dose of Prozac to a level at which it would control obsessive compulsive disorder. He developed diarrhea in addition to his now ever-present incontinence and attributed it to the Prozac. I reduced the dose. At forty milligrams a day, he was better. His obsessive compulsive symptoms almost disappeared after six weeks on this medicine.

Nonetheless, as his fears of AIDS and other mortal illnesses decreased, his incontinence increased. He became housebound and incontinent even at home. He said he had dozens of bowel movements a day, all with stool that he described as "little bits of pebbles." He felt bloated all the time. His gastroenterologist prescribed several anticholinergic medications to try to curb the bowel spasms that accompanied his bowel movements. Neither they nor a new trial of Thorazine helped.

Each time any of his physicians, myself included, brought one problem under control, Bill would develop a new one. I wondered whether Bill's incontinence and frequent bowel movements were psychologically induced. Did he have irritable bowel syndrome? I reconsidered his descriptions of his stools and their passage. These were not symptoms of ulcerative colitis. I recalled a childhood history of bowel symptoms before the onset of his ulcerative colitis.

I called the gastroenterologist and asked him to review all the X-ray films and results of bowel procedures. His very early investigation showed minimal evidence of ulcerative colitis, and in recent years there had been no evidence at all. Was the high dose of Prednisone treating Bill's symptoms rather than ulcerative colitis? Was his disability due in part to the debilitating side effects of Prednisone? Was the continuation of the steroid placating Bill's insistence on taking Prednisone because he feared a crash in mood if he discontinued it? Were his episodes of weight loss and fatigue part of a recurrent depressive disorder? If his symptoms were not related to ulcerative colitis, they might be psychologically induced—in which case, I knew I had to help Bill understand his relationship with his mother and how this influenced his symptoms. I had to share with him the insight that his bowel symptoms got worse when his obsessive compulsive disorder improved—that *symptoms* remained the channel through which he maintained close parental ties, never grew up, and never left home.

I did. He did not get angry, as he had done years before when I broached this same subject. He agreed with my assertions. A fruitful period of psychotherapy ensued.

At the same time, my questions set a process of diagnostic reevaluation in motion, because Bill's gastroenterologist was now receptive to considering different diagnoses, including irritable bowel syndrome—that is, somatization symptoms. The gastroenterologist prescribed an antispasmodic medication, and Bill improved. At the same time, he reduced his Prednisone slowly to twelve and a half milligrams.

Bill complained of feeling irritable, shaky, and exhausted as the

Prednisone was reduced. He admitted that he felt better physically, although he continued to have bowel symptoms.

"The only thing that's stopping me now is my head," he said. "I have cramps before going to a place like a restaurant. I feel like I have to go to the bathroom, and if I can't find one, I'm incontinent. This keeps me from getting a job. If that gets better, probably something else will crop up."

How right he was, I thought. As soon as one set of symptoms improved, another emerged. If he were well, he would have to leave home and lead a normal life. He was not yet ready to take this step.

Thus far, Bill had been diagnosed as suffering from ulcerative colitis, irritable bowel syndrome, obsessive compulsive disorder, major depression with delusions, and Prednisone-induced mood changes. I was about to make another diagnosis that I should have made long before.

Bill started to leave his house in the evenings and go to bars. He dated many young women. He often stayed out all night. "I don't need sleep anymore," he said. During the day, he was once more preoccupied, but not about disease. "I argue about politics. I'm angry all day. Do you know how committed I am? Once I learn something, it's there forever. I never make the same mistake twice. There isn't anything I can't understand. I'm brilliant."

Bill paused. I said nothing. It was one of those gratifying moments in the treatment of a highly complex patient when everything comes together for the psychiatrist. Sometimes it comes at the beginning of treatment; other times it takes longer. In Bill's case, it had taken many years, because he had drifted in and out of treatment and I had never been able to observe him for long periods. But now I could make the diagnosis that would have a tremendous impact on this young man's life. His lofty and exaggerated image of himself, his anger, his sleeplessness, and his increased sexual activity were the signs of manic depressive illness, a cyclical disorder. This was the first time I had observed him sufficiently to put together a picture of the mood cycles: depression, mania, and normal mood.

All along, I had searched for and found evidence of the depressive side. Although I had glimpsed the manic side years before, the episodes were too brief, not full-blown, and not fully revealed, because the patient did not stay in treatment continuously, interrupting it when he was "high." Bill had a number of episodes of mania, such as when he played varsity hockey on the college team despite serious physical illness and when he proclaimed his lofty ambitions after only a few days at an entry-level job. I realized that this treatment followed a pattern: he left when he was feeling good or "high" and came back when he was in a depressive phase. Somatization symptoms are not part of mania. The Prednisone had also obscured this diagnosis, because Bill would increase the dosage himself when he felt depressed and it elevated his mood.

I am always cautious and careful when I prescribe any medication. I had been especially so in Bill's case because of his physical symptoms. Now I felt I could proceed with a degree of confidence. Lithium is the usual treatment for manic-depressive illness. I persuaded him to try it and said that I would monitor him for side effects and watch the blood levels of the medicine scrupulously. He agreed to try it, and his response was sure and swift. His bowel symptoms remitted, to return only at times of increased stress.

Looking back, Bill Wallace's case is not a rare one. Many sufferers of somatization disorders have a lifetime of disability. It was only unusual because Bill had sought out psychiatric treatment, although he only did so for comfort and not a cure. Along with his other physicians, I took his complaints at face value. Any details Bill gave about his condition suited his need to maintain his illness. Therefore, I missed that he had manic episodes and they missed that he didn't have ulcerative colitis. How easily we physicians can be fooled. Ultimately, doctors are only as good as the information our patients give us.

Although Bill Wallace's diagnosis took many years to unfold, other patients may not require such prolonged investigation. His case was typical, though, of the way patients with somatization symptoms often interrupt or cut short their treatment. In light of this, the psychiatrist is always prepared to leave the door open for treatment in future times of need.

Bill's case was rewarding in other ways: he found a job, he got his own apartment, and moved on to independence and productivity. Even the self-centeredness—a cardinal trait of hypochondria—that had pervaded every aspect of his life diminished, and he was now able to express care and concern for others. His girlfriend left him. Instead of the self-absorbed, noncaring attitude I had come to expect, there was grief in Bill's voice and a tear in his eye.

·9·

Mirror, Mirror . . .

The word *milestone* is usually associated with major events in a child's development, when he or she first stands, talks, or is toilet trained. Some children "make their milestones" or achieve them ahead of expected time. Sometimes they lose their way. No one talks of adults making their milestones, although everyone knows that they do. Adults leave home, initiate intimate relationships, have children, send them off to be adults, age, and die. Along the way, between these major milestones, adults arrive at other signposts of development, at which, like children, they can get lost. They stand a greater chance of getting lost as adults if they also lost their way as children.

Birthdays that begin a decade represent an important adult milestone. Our moods, at such times, are mixed, containing elements of excitement and apprehension of the future, and nostalgia. The emotional impact of closing each decade and opening the next varies for individuals and between the sexes. Some take these milestones in stride, others don't even notice their passing, and still others are tortured by their advent.

Riva Cohen, a beautiful unmarried woman who appeared to be in her early thirties, belonged to the last category—although she was not aware of this. She recognized only events and feelings that spelled disaster for her. I knew, however, that her actions and emotions were related to events beginning in the present decade of her life.

Sometimes one hears the question "How can you be unhappy? You're so pretty." Riva Cohen's story could provide the answer. She was very pretty and very unhappy. In fact, the first thing she said to me that late-spring day when she appeared in my office was "Doctor, I'm so unhappy. I don't like myself."

Her dress contrasted with the styles I had just seen when I walked to my office. Young women, just like her, wore spring dresses. Riva was dressed in a stylish, simple, but somber and somewhat heavy dress. She wore no jewelry. Winter was still tugging at her; she wouldn't let it go.

Riva was slim and petite, her face small and heart shaped. Her skin was clear and pale. She seemed to wear no makeup. Her auburn hair was limp and dull. I pay attention to the way women care for their hair, because I have noticed that depressed women neglect it, and then wash and groom it as they recover.

Her small size, the too-obvious plainness of her dress, and her utter lack of adornment—she wore no rings or earrings—gave an overall impression of rigidity. The way she sat lent further strength to this impression. She hardly moved. She kept her legs demurely together, with the hem of her dress pulled halfway over her knees, like a convent school graduate. Altogether, a pretty girl, I thought, even if she didn't take full advantage of her attractiveness.

After her initial statement, Riva said nothing. This can also be a way of saying "I am unhappy. I don't like myself." It reveals nothing specific about the individual. Accordingly, a psychiatrist waits quietly to hear from the patient without actively soliciting details. This technique did not work with Riva. She said and did nothing but stare at the plant behind me.

After a period of uncomfortable silence, I felt constrained to ask, "Why are you so unhappy?"

"I don't know."

Silence. She clearly lacked spontaneity. I would need to work hard if she was going to reveal the source of her unhappiness and low self-esteem.

"Why did you want to see me?"

I asked the question in this way rather than saying "Why are you seeing me?" because I thought I could elicit history by demonstrating empathy. I anticipated that Riva, like most patients, had mulled and agonized over the decision to see a psychiatrist for some time. I hoped she would respond to this recognition by talking more openly. Had I asked the question in the second way, I might have given Riva an opportunity to reply with the short answer, "Things are not going well for me."

Silence. My empathic strategy had not worked. Because she had not yet expressed herself well verbally, I attempted to estimate her mood by observing physical clues and listening to the tone and pitch of her voice. I concluded that she looked sad and her voice was tinged with sullenness.

"Why don't you tell me about your life?" A general question and a further invitation to speak freely about anything that disquieted her.

Silence. My question must have been too general. I needed to be more specific.

"Tell me about your social life."

I assumed that a woman her age—early thirties—would regard her social life as important, and I must also have wondered what she thought about her age and single status.

"It's boring."

I didn't give up. "How do you spend your time in the evening?"

"I go to bars mainly. Usually with my girlfriends."

A long silence. More sullenness. A little irritability, too. I thought that perhaps talking about men was too difficult an area to start the interview. I decided to pursue a more neutral subject—girlfriends.

"Tell me about your friends."

"I don't have many. I have a roommate. I can't afford my own apartment. We share."

Silence.

"Where do you work?"

"I'm an administrative assistant at an ad agency. I've been there two years. It's okay."

This was a bit more than I'd been getting.

"What interests do you have?" I caught myself being too general again, and added, "How are your evenings spent when you don't go out?"

"I like music—rock. I sometimes go to the movies. I try to read. I usually don't finish the books I start, though."

Few interests. Did the fact that she didn't finish books mean she couldn't concentrate?

"I'm lonely."

Her first spontaneous sentence.

"It sounds like it. That must be one of the things that makes you so unhappy."

Another attempt at the empathy route.

"Yes."

This approach did not seem to be working now, but I did not give up. I gave it time.

"Do you have a family?"

"Yes. Until three years ago, I lived with my mother."

After a little wait. "Go on."

"She's in her late fifties. She remarried ten years ago. She's a weak person. She never gave me any direction. She's more a friend than a mother. I feel I'm weak because of her."

"Your father?"

"He left home when I was eighteen."

Were her thoughts slow and sparse because she was depressed? I thought I had better find out by asking some specific questions.

"How depressed do you feel?" (It would have been silly to ask "Are you depressed?")

"A lot. I'm so lonely."

"How are you sleeping?"

"Not well."

"Is the trouble falling or staying asleep?" In depressive disorder, people usually fall asleep easily, only to keep waking up throughout the night.

"Both."

"Are you eating well?" In depressive disorder, appetite is lost.

"Okay. I've gained weight."

"How are your bowels?" In depressive disorder, constipation is common.

"O.K."

No impressive symptoms of depressive disorder. On the other hand, she looked fairly depressed. She probably was. She seemed less irritated now. I decided to try returning to questions about the opposite sex. I was more direct this time.

"Are you dating?"

"Not really. Last time I dated was two to three years ago. I went out with someone for a few months. He was interested in me. I pulled away."

"Is it the lack of meaningful relationships that is depressing you?"

"I'm very upset about it. I would like to meet a man, get married, have children. Like everybody else."

She had hardly moved throughout the interview. I felt her tension, and it was taxing. We had come to the end of the session, and I said I felt it would be good for her to come again. She agreed.

What a curious session, I thought. Here was this pretty girl with a personality that was anything but pretty. I knew that she had to have a hard time finding dates. A man would have exhausted himself trying to engage her in any conversation. On the other hand, was she like this all the time? Was she worse now? Why had she come to see me now? Was she chronically withdrawn? Was I dealing with a schizoid personality—an isolated human being, uncomfortable with others, aloof and cold, and with a limited emotional range? I remembered the sullenness and irritability.

Riva had told me so little and, at times, even seemed resentful that I was asking. Here I was expressing interest and care, and she was reacting in this way. She made me angry; after all, she was seeking me out. How could I help her if she withheld even the most basic information from me?

I had disregarded her evasiveness during the session, but now I thought about it. During the interview, I had not given much weight to the suspicious side of her nature. She was a guarded person, not revealing more than she felt necessary. Was this a recent development in her personality? Was it a paranoid feature of depressive disorder? Her sleep was interrupted, but she was eating well. Was this an atypical depression in which the person is lethargic and withdrawn, stays in bed a lot, doesn't go out, over-eats, and gains weight?

I had no answers after that first meeting. I hoped that more would emerge at subsequent sessions. I planned to ask direct questions rather than open-ended ones.

At the beginning of our second session, Riva sat as quietly as she had before.

"What did you do this past weekend?" I asked.

"I did three things. One night, I went to the movies; one night, I went to a restaurant with some friends; one night, I went to the Italian festival in my neighborhood."

I continued to ask specific questions about how she had spent her time, thinking that this would be the most profitable approach.

"I spend a lot of time shopping for clothes. The ad agency I work for has a number of fashion houses as clients, so I can get my clothes for much less. It's important for me to look good."

After one long silence, Riva said, "I don't know what good it will do me to come here." She was to repeat this over again throughout the session, which made me rethink the likelihood of depressive disorder. On the other hand, it did not sound as though her energy levels were reduced, so I was not convinced that she had a depressive disorder.

Persisting in my direct approach, I managed to obtain a short history. Three years ago, Riva turned thirty, at which time she moved out of her mother's apartment. Two and a half years ago, she had a nose job. Two years ago, she changed jobs. A year ago, a dermatologist prescribed antibiotics and creams for her acne.

I thought I would test whether she was capable of psychological insight. "Do you think there may be psychological reasons for your loneliness and lack of success in your social life?"

The question irritated her. Her response was curt. "There's not a psychological reason for everything. I just feel bad."

I now had some insight into why Riva had come to see me. She was seeing a psychiatrist to ease her bad feelings, not because she wanted psychological insight.

She could not theorize about the psychological reasons for her unhappiness, but I could. When Riva reached thirty, a difficult milestone birthday for many women, she felt lonely and unhappy. She had not achieved her aims, to be married and have children. Ideas of time running out and dimmer prospects overwhelmed her. Introspection was not possible, so she decided that factors outside herself were inhibiting her goals and she would need to change them. She must have figured that she needed to take certain concrete steps to improve her life and chances to meet people and get married.

The first thing she did was to find her own apartment. When this made no difference, she decided to change jobs. When the people at her new job did not meet her expectations, she probably considered that she was not meeting people because her appearance was not as good as it should be. She had to improve her appearance. What was her weakest feature? She had always felt it was her nose. She had plastic surgery to make it perfect. She had always wanted to, anyway. When this, too, did not bring about the desired changes, she must have decided that perhaps her skin was not so attractive, either. She saw a dermatologist to take care of her skin. And, yes, she needed to dress well at all times. She therefore made use of her connections at work to get fine clothes inexpensively.

She had done all these things, and no change had occurred. I was reminded of people who pick up and move to California with the hope that their lives will be radically altered. Not that this doesn't work sometimes. But cosmetic changes didn't work for Riva. She was still her old self, whatever external changes were made. She was totally unaware that her inner world—her personality—and not her outer world—her appearance and the environment—was responsible for her loneliness.

But now she had exhausted the possibilities of social engineering to change her life. She was inundated with helplessness, frustration, and rage. What was the next available solution? I was not sure. Had it been depression? There was no evidence of depressive disorder. On the other hand, Riva had such a limited ability to express or distinguish among emotions, it was difficult to rule this out altogether. I had to wait to get further answers.

Under different circumstances, I would have approached this case with psychotherapy, using introspection to help the patient unravel the sources of her unhappiness and find more productive ways to deal with her predicament. In Riva's case, I thought this impossible. She was entirely outer directed. Her attempts to improve herself had never involved a "session with herself," an attempt to unravel the whys and wherefores of her emotional pain. Unlike most introspective individuals, she never used the word *because* followed by explanations, however inaccurate, in an effort to understand herself.

I decided that the preferred treatment for someone like Riva was medication. Medication would ease the pain without painful psychological probing. Although I did not have firm evidence for a diagnosis of depressive disorder, I thought of starting her on antidepressant medication but then decided to wait until I had more facts.

Three days later, Riva called. She was anxious to tell me what her "real" problem was. She sounded pressured.

"It's my nose."

I said nothing.

"My nose is not right. It has bumps. That's my real problem."

I did not know how to respond.

"I'm not coming back. The problem is my nose, and you can't fix that."

"I wish you would come back and tell me about it. I really have not had an opportunity to hear about this. While you are probably correct that I can't help your nose, I think you are depressed and we should talk about that and medicine, too."

I expected that having her return would require a great deal of persuasion, but it didn't.

Talk of Riva's nose dominated our next meeting. She was more spontaneous this time, although still vague and withholding. Her speech was pressured, as it had been on the telephone.

"It's hideous. My nose. It was ruined by my dermatologist. It was beautiful after the plastic surgery. Then I went to the dermatologist. He started me on all sorts of skin creams. This cleared up the pimples on my face. But the dermatologist didn't know that one of the creams causes funny lumps to develop on the nose after plastic surgery. Someone told me and I told the dermatologist. At first, he didn't believe me. Then he looked it up in the medical books. He found an article that proved I was right."

To prove her point, she handed me a copy of an article that did indeed discuss how a cream she had caused lumps after nasal plastic surgery—in a single case. But, much as I tried, I saw nothing amiss with her nose. I kept looking at it to reassure myself. It was beautiful. No lumps or bumps. It took awhile to understand the situation.

"It's ugly . . . ugly . . . ugly," she claimed.

I noticed that she had still not moved in the chair, maintaining her rigid pose, but she obviously felt freer to express some of her grief.

"It's ugly. Look at it. It's got bumps. It was so beautiful. I've been to see so many specialists. I've asked them to find out if there is anything to do about my nose. I want it corrected. The plastic surgeon won't even consider doing surgery again. I want him to. I must have gone to a dozen other plastic surgeons. None of them want to touch my nose. They don't believe me. I know better. The dermatologist made a mistake, and all the others are covering up for him."

There was a touch of haughtiness in this last statement.

"What do your friends think?" I asked.

"All of them think I'm crazy. I know I'm not. They say I have a beautiful nose. They are probably just trying to be nice to me because they know how bad I feel."

I now had an extension to my theory. She had not arrived at a solution to her predicament. Her mind had. In becoming psychotic, her real problems were temporarily laid to rest and alternative preoccupations were in force. The psychosis was not part of a depressive disorder—it was monosymptomatic hypochondriacal psychosis. That is, Riva was convinced that her nose was ugly and bumpy, despite all assertions to the contrary. Her convictions could not be shaken. She was delusional and, hence, by definition, psychotic. The delusion was restricted to only one aspect of her body, and, hence, was monosyptomatic.

I have seen a number of patents with this condition. I have seen quite acceptable noses regarded as hideous, and penises thought to be misshapen. The condition can also take other forms, the commonest of which is the belief that the skin is infested with worms or excoriating foreign bodies. A very handsome young man in his late teens complained to me that he had pronounced blue lines under his eyes and needed plastic surgery. I could not see these blue lines, nor could others. He, like many patients with monosymptomatic hypochondriacal psychosis, was ultimately successful in finding a plastic surgeon who would operate on his imagined defect.

Some patients are firmly convinced that they emit foul odors from the mouth or anus. One middle-aged woman, a telephone operator, swore she passed gas the whole day and her coworkers smelled her all the time.

"How did they manage to stay in the same room as you?" I asked. "Surely they smelled you all the time and objected."

"They never complained," she answered. "They probably didn't know it was me, or were too embarrassed to say anything, or they didn't want to hurt me."

One case, which I always qualify by saying it is a true story, involved a sixteen-year-old, good-looking, intelligent patient named Leo. He complained to a gastroenterologist that the FBI had placed an electronic device in his mouth while he slept. The bug was now in his alimentary tract. In this way, the FBI always knew of his whereabouts. (The self-importance of the deluded is both comical and sad.) The bug was giving him abdominal cramps and diarrhea. The gastroenterologist, not one to suggest psychiatric intervention, decided on his own creative course of action. He saw Leo weekly and examined his bowel under X-ray fluoroscopy. Each week, the doctor reassured him that the bug had moved farther down his bowel and would soon be excreted. On the sixth week, the doctor announced, "It's out. I can't see it anymore. You've passed it." The following week the patient returned with the news: "The FBI found out that I passed their bug and put a new one in me." At that point, the gastroenterologist referred Leo to me.

Monosymptomatic hypochondriacal psychosis is not associated with any other psychiatric disorder. Although those that have it have feelings of depression, they do not have depressive disorder. As with Riva, a schizoid personality style is common and interpersonal difficulties of a serious nature are the rule. Insomnia is frequent, and so is suspiciousness. Shame is also frequent and may inhibit full disclosure, as it did with Riva. Because of their insistence on having a physical disorder, these patients undergo extensive medical investigation and treatment. Like Riva, they become angry over their physicians' incompetence.

I thought that I would wait another week before offering her Pimozide, a specific medication for monosymptomatic hypochondriacal psychosis.

I used the time between sessions to give further thought to her psychological life, but I made only slight progress. I wondered about Riva's passive mother, whom she accused of making her weak. Was this just another person, an outer object, to blame for her unhappiness? Or did her mother's inadequacy contribute to Riva's inability to deal with life's milestones in a productive, introspective, and contemplative way? Or both?

When the quality of the mother-child relationship is good, the child is more likely to negotiate developmental milestones successfully. One of the most important of these milestones is separation from the mother. As we have noted, when this is successfully accomplished, the child develops an adequate sense of self and a fantasy life, both of which encourage later introspection and the expression of feeling states in verbal rather than physical language.

Another young woman with Riva's predicament would have tried to understand something of the problem and its possible causes. She would have shared her thoughts and feelings with others, and, in so doing, further refined her insights. Then she would have taken appropriate actions to master the problems. These actions might have included *some* of the external changes Riva tried.

When the milestone of separation and individuation is not adequately negotiated in childhood, two situations develop. First, feeling states tend to be expressed in physical language, as in the various forms of hypochondria. Second, the cause of one's problems is seen to lie exclusively outside of oneself. Riva exhibited both of these features. She could find no language to express her feeling state other than the words "I'm feeling bad." Her "bad" feelings were, in turn, expressed through a physical preoccupation, her delusion about her nose. Her lack of fantasy life, shown in the sparseness of her language, lack of emotion, and emptiness, did not allow for more creative solutions to her predicament.

Riva returned to the fourth session, announcing that it would be her last. She said that she felt attached to me and wanted to stop seeing me. This acknowledgment of how she responded to what must have been the earliest feelings of affection offered further evidence of why she had not established any significant relationships and why she was so lonely.

I thought that there was another reason she could not continue seeing me. If her "ugly" nose was not her problem, she might have been forced to acknowledge emotional causes for her troubles. I doubted that Riva could have borne this or dealt with it.

I was not surprised, therefore, when she also rejected my offer of Pimozide.

PART THREE

...

A Romance with Illness

·10·

The Incredible
Munchausens

The young man had been in an automobile accident two years before and lost much of the skin on his lower left leg as a result. Since then, the plastic surgeon had performed a series of skin grafts using skin from other parts of the patient's body to repair the leg. The grafts refused to heal and became infected. The surgeon ascribed their failure to "take" to insufficient splinting after the surgeries, and he encased the leg in a plaster cast. This made no difference. The leg did not heal and remained infected. Now it was black and gangrenous. The usually calm and unflappable surgeon, unable to explain why this was happening, turned angry and frustrated. To control the gangrene and provide enough blood to the leg to encourage healing, he created a channel of skin and tissue between the right and left legs. This, too, became infected. He brought in specialists to see whether the patient's immune system was out of kilter and therefore rejected the new tissue—even though it was the patient's own. All their tests came back negative.

The patient threatened to sue the surgeon and the hospital for malpractice. After rounds one morning, one of his residents asked, "Do you think the patient could be undoing the surgery and infecting it himself?"

"I don't believe that," the surgeon snapped. "No one in his right mind would do that."

The surgeon's rejection of the idea that someone would harm himself in such a perverse way was shared by television journalist Barbara Walters. She echoed the surgeon's words when she heard the story of a mother whom doctors accused of deliberately creating life-threatening illnesses in her baby and who, in turn, accused doctors of victimizing her.

The skin graft patient who repeatedly ripped apart and infected his wounds had Munchausen syndrome, or factitious disorder. So, too, did the mother who laced her baby's milk with harmful medications. Because she harmed another rather than herself, she was a Munchausen by proxy.

People with intermittent somatization symptoms or hypochondria *believe* they have physical illness. People with Munchausen syndrome *create* physical illness in themselves. They do this to avoid emotional discomfort, particularly the psychic pain generated by the anticipation of loss.

Munchausens devote all or a major portion of their lives to creating physical illness and the illusion that they have physical illness by intentionally inflicting injury, pain, and suffering on themselves. They have repeated surgery and invasive diagnostic procedures, usually followed by complications much in excess of the expected. They take as many medicines as they can get their hands on, the higher the dosage the better. In effect, they are drug addicts.

Munchausen syndrome is an extreme illness. Its sufferers exhibit extreme behavior, emotional fluctuations, and attitudes. They provoke extreme feelings in those with whom they come in contact.

Munchausen syndrome is incurable.

Patients with somatization symptoms may invoke incredulity in family, friends, and physicians because their convictions that they have physical illness are at odds with the scientific evidence. But, no person with somatization symptoms, however severe their symptoms, however chronic their condition, stimulates the degree of disbelief engendered by patients with Munchausen syndrome.

Munchausen patients are aware of what they are doing but

cannot stop themselves. Their actions are conscious, but the motivation is unconscious and out of their control. They behave as if their lives depended on having continuous medical illness, and they pursue their goal of manufacturing and simulating disease with unremitting vigor. Their tactics may be simple or complex but are always devious. For example, they may feign a fever by putting a thermometer on a heater or actually create a fever by infecting themselves with a dirty needle. They may feign bladder disease by pricking their fingers and contaminating their urine samples with their blood or create bladder disease by putting sharp objects into the urethra.

Munchausen patients lie with impunity and avoid exposure artfully. They present their medical histories with dramatic flair, in the vaguest possible terms, yet sufficiently detailed to intrigue doctors and trigger repetitive diagnostic tests. Skilled manipulators, they require the unwitting collusive commitment of their doctors to maintain the illusion of grave infirmity; they accept the prospect of and endure painful invasive procedures stoically. Munchausen patients do not acknowledge that theirs is an emotional disorder.

In medicine, the illness is the culprit and the patient is the victim. Munchausens make themselves rather than their illnesses the enemies of physicians, all the while displaying an insatiable need to maintain ongoing relationships with them. The only people of major importance in their lives, in fact, are the medical professionals who test and treat them. Their life stories are embellished with episodes of tragic loss to elicit sympathy and extra care. They are isolated individuals, family and friends having long since withdrawn their support and sympathy.

Hospitals—they go from one to another—are their primary residences, providing sanctuaries from the ever-looming emotional pain that the stresses of life promise. When admitted, Munchausen patients complain of extensive pain and demand painkillers. Their hospital stays are frequent, protracted, and, more often than not, exceed the norms for their alleged conditions. When threatened with discovery or discharge, they have been known to rush from the hospital, clad in pajamas and attached to an IV, to hail a taxi.

As patients, they are demanding and provocative, instigating disagreements among staff members and terrorizing other patients by planting seeds of doubt and distrust in their minds. When presented with the lack of hard evidence of their medical illnesses or when confronted with the part they played in producing them, they rage uncontrollably, protest raucously, and threaten malpractice suits. When told they will be discharged after an extensive workup has yielded only negative findings, they aggravate their existing conditions or produce new sets of symptoms in order to prolong their stay or gain admission to another hospital. Munchausens always pose as victims.

Their behavior diminishes the possibility of their leading productive lives. Some hold jobs and have families, but their absenteeism is high and their home life chaotic. Some work sporadically, keeping their jobs long enough to make them eligible for health insurance. Sometimes they simply fabricate their insurance coverage, duping doctors and hospitals into believing they are well covered. Others, as invalids, manage to manipulate the system and get government health insurance. One patient, "paralyzed" in both legs and one arm, came to the hospital accompanied by around-the-clock companions who were all paid by government agencies. When one of the companions took a break, a ward nurse saw the patient get out of bed and go to the bathroom.

Munchausen patients amass an unusually complete knowledge of medicine to help them create imitations of everyday and rare medical illnesses. They read medical texts and journals religiously. With a talent for using this knowledge to fool physicians, Munchausen patients are consummate actors. Unlike professional performers, however, they cannot distinguish between real life and the play, and the play becomes the thing. They know they are performing, but they cannot help themselves. Like the professional actors that medical schools employ to act out illness for students, Munchausen patients also receive their training from medical professionals. The majority have, at some point in their lives, worked in a medically related field where they have had an opportunity to learn and hone their medical skills. I have known practicing physicians, medical and nursing students, nurses, medical receptionists, ambulance drivers, paramedics, and aides who were Munchausens.

Munchausen patients make societal issues part of their personal victimhood. In the course of a television talk show, a young woman described how she had stood in front of a mirror and cut out her own inflamed tonsils, bit by bit, with a pair of scissors and without painkillers. The incredulous talk-show host wanted to know why she performed her own tonsillectomy. The young woman answered that she had no medical insurance and could not afford doctor's fees.

There are no statistics for this illness. Reluctance to accept the notion that an individual might resort to self-injury in an attempt to provoke medical illness accounts, in part, for infrequent accurate diagnosis and a subsequent underestimated incidence of Munchausen syndrome. Those familiar with the illness agree that its incidence is probably much higher than usually acknowledged. The patients' need to hide the true nature of their illnesses contributes to the absence of statistics for this condition. In addition, little corroborative or conflicting history is available, because so few family members and friends visit them when they are hospitalized, and because they usually refuse to allow their physicians to contact family members. Many, in fact, depict themselves as orphans. This also leads to underdiagnosis of Munchausen syndrome.

The name Munchausen syndrome was given the condition in 1951 by the English physician Richard Asher, who found these patients' histories so outlandish he was prompted to recall the tales of the real-life Baron Karl von Münchhausen. Münchhausen was a German nobleman (1720–97), who is said to have wandered the German countryside regaling travelers with outrageous, uproarious, and blatantly untrue tales of his derring-do. Although there really was a Baron von Münchhausen, the stories attributed to him derive from many sources in many countries. They were initially published in English in 1875 and later translated into German.

In America, the Munchausen name passed into English via the fast-talking radio comedian Fritz Perl, who affected a German accent and appropriated the name for his 1940s radio character. The actual tales were brought to the public's attention again in the 1980s with Terry Gilliam's film *The Adventures of Baron*

Munchausen. These popularizations, however, had nothing to do with the illness.

Asher was not the first physician to recognize Munchausen syndrome or single out its victims. Healers in the Middle Ages described "hysterics" who produced bloody sputum by placing leeches in their mouths or excoriated their skins to produce lesions. In 1843, the physician Gavin distinguished those who sought to gain compensation or advance their position by simulating illness. He described them as malingerers and could find no acceptable explanation for their behavior other than a need to deceive. In 1934, Karl Menninger recognized this group of patients and called them "polysurgical addicts" because they seemed to have insatiable cravings for surgery.

Munchausen patients have been called hospital hobos, hospital addicts, peregrination problem patients, and hospital black book patients, a reference to the register some hospitals maintain to recognize and bar these patients from their beds. Because the more chronic among them wander from hospital to hospital, the illness has been romanticized and called Ahasveras (wandering Jew) syndrome.

Although the lives of Munchausen patients are real, bleak, painful, and anything but romantic, the Munchausen patient carries on a romance with illness. Behind the horror and exaggeration is an infatuation with illness that begins in childhood and endures a lifetime.

Not so long ago, like the plastic surgeon and the talk-show host, I also would have found Munchausen syndrome and Munchausen by proxy incredible. But my experience directing a psychiatric ward for patients with major medical and psychiatric illness—a psych-med unit—educated me in the ways of Munchausen patients. Many of the patients we admitted had presented their physicians with insoluble diagnostic riddles for years. Many were Munchausen patients. To this day, however, I cannot say that my education in this area has been complete. Each time I think I know how a Munchausen creates an illness, I am confronted with a new, more startling method. Any studies I have tried to make of these patients have always been complicated by their peripatetic ways and rejection of psychiatric intervention.

In the pages that follow, we enter the world of Munchausen patients to the degree that they allow us. We consider the means they use to get to their ends, and we see how they interact with medical personnel, family, and friends. Explanations are given of how the illness may begin, and its moral, legal, and economic ramifications are considered. Actual case studies show how Munchausen patients carry on their romance with illness and, in the process, terrorize the medical world.

· 11 ·

The World of the Munchausen

The Munchausen's romance with illness is not true love. The Munchausen's affairs are one-sided and devoid of sexuality. They court illness because they develop so great a sensitivity to emotional pain, they are prepared to make extreme sacrifices to avoid it. They constantly invite death, going to the edge of the precipice and then exhorting their physicians to take extraordinary measures to save their lives.

Physicians play an essential and enduring role in the Munchausen's romance with illness. On the surface, the patient appears to be carrying on a romance with the physician, but going beneath the veneer we see that the physician is really the matchmaker, pairing the patient with a partner—a diagnosed illness—and introducing new ones until the right one is found. Although the physician may not be the primary object of the patient's obsessive infatuation, the relationship (a word I use hesitantly because of its hollowness in this case) between the patient and physician is of paramount importance in the genesis and maintenance of the disorder.

Munchausen patients can create facsimiles of any illness from the common to the rare. Equally as important, their symptoms never completely conform to standards. When I dared suggest a diagnosis of Munchausen syndrome in a patient with uveitis (an inflammation of the iris) whose origins could not be accounted for, her perplexed physician replied almost without hesitation: "This patient can't have Munchausen syndrome because Munchausen patients never get uveitis." His response was reflexive—and inaccurate. His answer told me he had been hooked. Munchausen patients can mimic any illness, and it turned out that this patient, a medical student and daughter of a pharmacist, had been putting cell-wall-hardening drops in her eyes since childhood. I later learned that my colleague knew something, but not too much, about Munchausen syndrome and had never seen an actual case. I could not fault him; not too many physicians have, and when they do, they often cannot be persuaded that Munchausen syndrome is a real diagnosis. In this instance, the doctor became convinced when the patient left the eyedrops in the bathroom, where they were found by an alert aide.

The question I am asked most often about Munchausen patients is: "How do they do it?" The medical student's methodology was relatively simple and, indeed, Munchausen patients often do no more than overuse medications to create their conditions. More often, their creativity knows no bounds.

Patients add sugar to urine samples and send their doctors on the trail of diabetes. They come into emergency rooms or doctors' offices with symptoms of kidney stones: acute pain, fever, vomiting, difficulty passing urine, blood in the urine. The symptoms, of course, have "passed" by the time a doctor sees them, but an entry of kidney stones is made in their charts. The next time they have an attack, their symptoms will be more apparent because they have contaminated their urine with blood, their own or that of an animal.

They puzzle dermatologists with the sores, rashes, and lesions they create by exposure to ice or chemical irritants. They abrade their skin with sandpaper to produce eczema-like conditions. One patient simply rubbed her eyelids with her hands to the point of ulceration and then infected the sores. After plastic surgeons repaired the damage, the patient irritated her wounds again and stimulated a new round of surgery.

Not content with sticking their fingers down their throats, Munchausen patients induce vomiting by drinking corrosive substances that also may erode the lining of their throats and stomachs, creating additional symptoms.

Knowing that doctors regard unexplained or unusual bleeding as a danger signal, they induce it when they can. They take anticoagulant medicine to produce hemorrhages.

By taking gross doses of laxatives, adding blood to their stool specimens, or inserting sharp objects up their rectums, Munchausen patients seduce their physicians into diagnoses of colitis or ileitis. This may lead to surgical procedures, a colostomy or ileostomy in which the bowel is brought out on the abdominal wall and drains into a pouch. There are always complications; for instance, I discovered one patient using a sharpened pencil to tamper with the exposed bowel and give the impression that the colitis had spread to the remaining sections of intestine and bowel, which would have necessitated more surgery.

Because starvation lowers the body's ability to resist infection, this becomes a surefire method of inducing disease. Munchausen patients, having supplemented starvation diets with large doses of diuretics and laxatives, and after self-induced vomiting, are brought to the hospital barely alive and given intravenous feedings of life-saving protein supplements. Once saved, they contaminate the intravenous lines and induce septicemia.

They confound cardiologists with signs of heart disease because they have taken medications that give them anginal pain, irregular heart rhythms, and enlarged hearts. They perplex neurologists by feigning epileptic seizures or inducing them with drugs.

I have rarely met a Munchausen patient who at some time or another did not appear to have lupus erythematosus, a serious autoimmune disorder that affects the connective tissue. It fits right into the Munchausen syndrome, because the blood test for lupus is not specific to the disorder and is positive in many people who take a variety of drugs, as of course the Munchausen patient does. Moreover, because steroids are the treatment of choice for lupus and steroids have side effects, the Munchausen patient accepts the prescription, promptly abuses it, and reports to a new doctor with allegations of a different illness (really the side effects of the steroids).

They manage to baffle psychiatrists, too. Reluctant to see us when Munchausen syndrome is suspected, they may mimic the symptoms of other psychiatric disorders, which is relatively easy because of the subjective nature of psychiatric complaints. They also overdose on psychoactive drugs that induce delirium, delusions, and hallucinations. They end up on psychiatric wards because frazzled hospital administrators, desperate to get them off the medical-surgical wards, often give Munchausen patients the option of being transferred to a psychiatric ward or being discharged.

The answer to the question of how Munchausens do it is: just about any way they can. However, understanding what Munchausen syndrome is and how Munchausen patients create illness does not smooth the way for dealing with these patients. This is difficult, if not impossible. They challenge physicians at every turn, beginning with a doctor's natural reluctance to accept that the devastation these patients perpetrate on themselves is predominantly the product of the unconscious mind and out of the patient's control. Doctors want to help their patients; helping patients includes making a diagnosis, and the Munchausen patient, replete with symptoms, begs to be given a medical diagnosis. By withholding information, the patient lulls the doctor into believing that the presenting symptoms of the moment, no matter how obscure, represent a singular and total illness; this is a situation and a concept with which most physicians can deal because we expect illness to manifest itself this way.

A perusal of Munchausen patients' hospital charts reveals the names of illnesses that are rare to the point of nonexistence. Many are preceded by the adjective *idiopathic,* meaning no known cause. Moreover, the charts show that each consultant views these patients in a light consonant with his or her own specialty and refers to different bodies of medical literature. A patient with low blood pressure described as "idiopathic" had an encyclopedic chart bulging with articles from vascular, neurological, cardiological, and nutritional journals in many languages. Each described a rare case that almost, but not completely, matched this patient's circumstances. Moreover, the diagnosis of a rare disease can represent a triumph for the physician and a "victory" for the patient; but in the process of arriving at this diagnosis, the true nature of the patient's problem is further obscured.

The dependence of Munchausen patients on physicians and their interactions with them is illustrated by a patient I saw who could not eat without vomiting. Her doctors thought she had bowel paralysis and diagnosed her as having a rare condition of the bowel. (Only later did we find out that she was also infecting her intravenous lines and overdosing on diuretics.) Several treatments were tried, and although her physician did not suspect any psychiatric illness, he decided to try another approach, a tranquilizer that might reverse the bowel paralysis, and he wanted to know if I thought this course of treatment was advisable. However, as a psychiatrist who had the potential for unearthing the truth about this patient, I also had the potential for wrecking the patient's relationship with her doctor.

Meeting with the patient, I said little to reveal that I knew from my review of her charts and discussions with her physicians that she took diuretics and had a history of repeated hospitalizations. Nor did I let on that I suspected she was factitiously engineering her symptoms. Nonetheless, she appeared to know my thoughts: Munchausen patients seem to have uncanny abilities to read minds, and they rely on this skill to monitor their doctor's reactions.

From the start, this patient was furious and uncommunicative with me. It was clear that I was an interloper threatening to break up her relationship with her doctor, and knowing how much he meant to her, I almost wanted to say that I was sorry. I need not have worried; she was not going to let me have my say. When I followed up the next day, I saw a note in her chart saying that she now had low blood pressure. I thought this unusual, and when I spoke to her physician, he said, "I know what you are saying, but she has real disease." He went on to explain that he had discovered some obscure cause for this latest complication. In fact, her low blood pressure was caused by the diuretics she was secretly taking. This doctor had been ensnared and could not get out of his patient's trap.

This case presents a classic example of how Munchausen patients manipulate physicians into pursuing the investigation of their illness by constantly instilling doubt in doctors' minds. This keeps physicians drawing fine lines between the acceptance or rejection of the presence of illness.

Munchausen patients deceive their doctors in many other ways. For example, they may assume the identities of famous people and recreate situations from their lives. A blind man told the staff that he was a defrocked priest whose eyes had been put out by a jealous lover following a sexual escapade—shades of Oedipus Rex. He wore a priest's cossack and hobbled around the ward with a cane fashioned from a gnarled branch. He held his eyes tightly shut, but every so often the nurses saw him open them when he lit a cigarette. The nursing staff also observed that he opened his eyes at times when walking and knew exactly what he was doing.

Munchausen patients use any means, including sexual, to seduce a doctor into doing more medical investigations. Female patients on hospital wards often choose sheer nightgowns with plunging necklines; not only do many female Munchausen patients prefer this type of lingerie, they also expose their genitals. Because emotionally intact women rarely do this, the female Munchausen's lack of propriety is striking; it is especially so with a psychiatrist, because the patient knows that he is not going to do a physical examination. Not surprisingly, many female Munchausen patients tell of being molested and raped by their physicians. Because Munchausen patients are notorious liars and manipulators, many if not most of these stories of sexual abuse by physicians are not credible. Whatever their overt suggestions of sexuality, both male and female Munchausen patients have highly restricted sexual interests and limited sexual experience. Their sexually seductive behavior is not based on true mutual feeling or mature sexuality. It is yet another ploy to engage physicians in a pursuit of the causes of their illnesses.

In their interaction with physicians, Munchausen patients seem to be recreating parental relationships that were either all-caring or all-rejecting. They invite their physicians to enter into arrangements in which the doctors' identities are split into parts that are either all-nurturing or all-rejecting. Initially, each physician represents a nurturing parental figure, the giver of unconditional love. In the Munchausen patient's terms, this means acknowledging and enabling the presence of serious physical illness and pursuing its diagnosis and treatment. As long as the doctor believes the patient has genuine illness and pursues its diagnosis, the patient regards him as caring. When the doctor begins to doubt that medical illness exists but continues the investigation, the patient becomes alarmed, fearing that the care will stop, but does not give up hope it will continue. When the doctor ends the evaluation, he is now, in the patient's opinion, rejecting.

If the physician responds with rage upon learning an illness was self-induced or mimicked, the Munchausen's belief that the physician/parent doesn't care is justified. It is as though Munchausens are saying, "See, I knew all along you were just out to hurt me. Now I have proof."

Munchausen patients project their sadism, and their identities as both patient and medical expert, onto their physicians by continually and viciously taunting, teasing, and fooling them with new symptoms and complications. And, through this process of projecting their traits and identities onto others, these patients assume that the person wearing the white coat, stethoscope in pocket, is a fellow sadist.

With their dual identities of suffering patient and medical expert, Munchausen patients vacillate between ceding total control to their doctors and taking power. They masochistically allow doctors to invade their bodies without question or restriction, then tamper with the results. They provide the physicians with clues, challenging them to guess whether the whole thing is a ruse. When the truth starts to dawn on doctors and they exercise their powers to cease the investigations and discharge these patients from their care, the Munchausen creates new symptoms to regain control.

Munchausen patients invariably expose their feigning and self-induced illnesses. They often leave syringes lying around, allow themselves to be observed warming thermometers, conceal their personal stores of pills poorly, or are caught stealing hospital charts and drugs. Tales of doctors who have cracked cases of Munchausen syndrome abound in hospital mythologies.

One distinguished colleague's name was always mentioned with particular reverence because of one rather infamous case he had solved. The patient in question had very low blood sugar and the symptoms of hypoglycemia: sweatiness, racing pulse, fainting spells. She was hospitalized for weeks, during which time tests for the cause of her symptoms proved negative. Frustrated, her physicians brought in a surgeon who was ready to "open her up and take a look at her pancreas." He thought that she might have insulinoma, a tumor on the pancreas that stimulates insulin secretion and consequently low blood sugar. On the day of surgery, the surgeon decided to search the patient's bed locker. He found syringes and insulin. The patient was injecting herself with insulin. She was discharged. No one ever dared remind him that what had led him to search her locker was simply her carelessness. When he had visited her the day before, she had left a syringe and bottle of insulin in full view on her night table.

The need to hold on to the relationship is not exclusively the patients'. Physicians have a need to maintain doctor-patient relationships and build strong and enduring personal bonds with their patients. Most patients appreciate this and respect their doctors for it. Munchausen patients, however, use this relationship as a potent means of maintaining the illusion that they have serious illness. It allows them the opportunity to perpetually create new illnesses for investigation. Why would a doctor prolong such a relationship? The reasons are varied. Most physicians, by nature and training, are caring. They derive their gratification from taking responsibility and helping others. They feel unhappy, even guilty, when they cannot help a patient. Munchausen patients are expert when it comes to raking up these emotions in their physicians. Additionally, doctors are trained to pursue diagnosis and feel inadequate when they cannot arrive at one.

Having established a positive friendship with their primary physician, Munchausen patients take to alienating consulting specialists, nurses, social workers, and others involved in their cases. While welcoming the primary physician, the patients remain uncommunicative with others; they may openly tell visiting consultants that their diagnoses are inadequate or roll their eyes and make clucking sounds to demonstrate their distaste for an opinion. They may lock themselves in the bathroom and keep consultants waiting; or they may tell the nursing staff how poorly doctors have treated them, often lying about what these physicians have said. For instance, patients may falsely allude to a doctor's sexual interest in them, enthusiasm for performing unnecessary surgery, or love of money.

They turn their care givers into hawks and doves, setting one group against the other. The doves feel sympathetic to the patients' plight and demonstrate their sympathies with tests and procedures—way beyond the expected and necessary. The hawks are skeptical, dubious, and suspicious of the patients' diagnoses. They urge caution and restraint. When a hawkish physician broaches the possibility that the patient is suffering from Munchausen syndrome, the dovish members of the medical staff say: "How could you imply that this poor, suffering soul is doing this to himself?" or "How could you think he is faking it?" The field is set for a tournament between the "nasties and negligents" and the "caring and sympathetic." If one camp infuses doubt in the other, the latter goes to inordinate lengths to avoid the possibility of oversight or negligence. Each side is set to wondering whether something has been overlooked. Nurses, medical students, residents, and outside consultants are all engaged in debates over the "right" course of treatment. No one wins.

Medical staffs aren't the only groups caught in the Munchausen patients' webs. Families unite with their offspring against doctors, accusing them of ineptitude because they cannot find the causes of the illnesses. Such behavior really is a continuation of patterns established early in the Munchausen patients' childhoods. Mrs. P. was convinced her daughter, Isabel, had ileitis because the young woman had already been in treatment for several years. When I suggested that Isabel's illness was factitious, the mother was openly hostile. She asked, "Do you think all those doctors have been treating her for ileitis for all these years for nothing? You're the expert and they're the idiots. Right?"

Although she came around to see that many of the other illnesses her daughter suffered from were factitious, Isabel's mother never really accepted the notion that her daughter did not have genuine ileitis. Instead, the mother adopted another technique to prove her point: she cross-examined me with prosecutorial zeal. When I was unable to answer all her questions and solve all the mysteries of her daughter's condition, the woman smiled victoriously. I realized that by asking me so many questions I could not answer, she was mocking me.

Even on those rare occasions when the patient does accept the diagnosis, the family may reject it. I saw a young woman, a nursing student, who at age twenty already had an extensive history of self-mutilation and factitious illnesses. She told me that she knew her diagnosis. She asked me to tell her parents about her illness, hoping that they would arrange long-term hospitalization for her—an obvious bonanza for a Munchausen patient. I approached the family and shared my conclusions, only to find myself being accused of cruelty. They wished that I were lying; by telling the truth I had robbed them of their hopes. I tried to dam up my own emotions, aware of what parents must feel when they discover that their child has this bizarre illness for which there is no treatment.

As I have mentioned, families and friends usually give up on these patients, even when they don't know the true diagnosis. The physician who raises the possibility of Munchausen syndrome to a patient's family at an early stage—or at just about any point—is like a quarterback throwing an incomplete pass, because rather than catch the ball and deal with the diagnosis, the most devoted families become overwhelmed, frustrated, and alienated—and finally abandon the patient to medical surrogates. Indeed, experienced Munchausen patients have no visitors in the hospital.

In addition to difficulties with the medical establishment and their own families, Munchausen patients pose ethical dilemmas that impact on society as a whole. Hospitals exist to treat the sick; but when it comes to Munchausen patients, some institutions draw the line and keep their names and photographs in files labeled DO NOT ADMIT. But Munchausen patients are seriously ill, albeit by their own hands, and require admission most of the time. This situation is further complicated by the Munchausens' predilection for threatening and initiating malpractice suits. Just as they devour medical texts, they scour law journals for stories of malpractice suits that could be formats for their own legal actions.

Hospitals and physicians can find themselves caught between a desire to expose Munchausen patients and issues of confidentiality. Hospitals circulate the identities of these patients, and doctors publish frank reports that name Munchausen patients and end with admonitions like "This case is reported in the hope that it will lead to [patient's name]'s rapid recognition in the case of future hospital presentations" or "Mr. X is still at large—he may impersonate you next."

The argument can be made that doctors have an obligation to prevent patients from hurting themselves and therefore should expose Munchausen patients for their own good. Exposing a Munchausen's fraudulent activities may also be the right thing to do. On the other hand, these exposures involve a violation of patient-doctor confidentiality. In reality, any publicity has done little to curb the activities of Munchausen patients, because most require emergency admission and their doctors are so busy caring for them that they have no time to check their histories.

The cost of caring for Munchausen patients has not been calculated; we don't even know how many there are. My guess is that there are many, and society foots the bill.

The question that still begs to be answered is "Why?" Clearly, Munchausen patients do not want psychiatrists to probe their illness too deeply, and they subvert our efforts at every turn by lying or running away from close scrutiny. They keep families at a distance, fearing that they might provide unwelcome clues to their character. They scrutinize their own charts and steal them when they find even the slightest suggestion of a diagnosis of factitious disorder or Munchausen syndrome.

What we know about Munchausen syndrome derives from the

whole body of psychiatric knowledge. We make our assumptions because Munchausen patients exhibit features of many psychiatric disorders, although the sum of Munchausen syndrome is greater than any of its psychiatric components. The questions one must ask about Munchausen syndrome are: Why does the attempt to avoid emotional discomfort lead to Munchausen syndrome? Why are these patients so masochistic? Why is their masochism directed toward the creation of illness? Why is their only permanent identity that of patients?

There are no easy answers, just hypotheses.

About the only theory I can accept with some certainty is that creating and feigning illness as a way of life is the Munchausen patients' attempt, however bizarre, to overcome the stresses of life and insulate themselves from them. It is an attempt to master their inner sense of having no control by trying to control their outer world in a perverse way. Although all stress and the emotional discomfort it causes have a major impact on these patients, the stress of *loss* looms grotesquely larger than any other.

Other factors, however, linked to childhood experiences, may contribute to the development of a Munchausen personality. When something goes amiss in the early mother-infant relationship, it may entrench an inherited tendency to an abnormal personality style and impede the development of a firm sense of self and, therefore, of fixed identity. Chameleonlike, they adopt the identities of others. In addition, their lack of separateness leads to an inability to be alone and self-reliant. They also develop an exaggerated sense of entitlement. Such people see the world in extremes, cannot distinguish between right and wrong, and cannot control their wild and sudden emotional swings. Most importantly for Munchausens, this early failure in personality development makes them hypersensitive to the trauma of loss. Thus they interpret *any* deprivation of the mother's care as if they were going to lose her. When the mother's attention is focused on a new baby or a sick sibling, the Munchausen reacts catastrophically. Under the stress, they become physically ill. The mother's withdrawal has become synonymous with loss and illness, and the equation LOSS = ILLNESS is permanently fixed in the older child's mind.

It is remarkable how many adult Munchausen patients tell stories of recent deaths of spouses, parents, and children. Even if these events are fabricated, their telling substantiates the critical part loss plays in their lives. Moreover, any loss of a loved one is almost invariably followed by symptoms that rekindle the doctor-patient relationship, suggesting that physicians are viewed as substitutes for their lost loved ones.

Two other factors are critical in the development of the Munchausen's personality: child abuse and a distorted perception of early medical care or hospitalizations. Incidents of abuse are repeated in chilling detail. They may well be true in some cases but not in all; the incidents are often convincingly refuted by parents and relatives. Perhaps the most important aspect of their histories of abuse is that most patients perceived them that way, irrespective of whether they occurred. Whatever the case, the child's perception of abuse is a precedent for masochistic behavior in the future.

Another precedent for this kind of behavior is identification with an abused parent. One mother of a Munchausen patient told me that she lived for twelve years married to a man who beat her constantly, cheated on her, and even brought his adolescent sexual partners home. After impregnating a fifteen-year-old, the man left home. The mother dated a lawyer, who wanted to marry her; when her husband came home and begged forgiveness, she turned the lawyer down and took the husband in again. The daughter, the Munchausen patient, had identified with her abused mother by abusing herself through the creation of serious illness. As her father punched her mother, the patient beat her abdomen until it was so bruised that her surgeon took the abdominal tenderness as a sign of peritonitis and operated.

Another verifiable defining event in a Munchausen patient's life is an illness in early childhood that required hospitalization or intensive medical care. Both patient and parent always remember the incident, but with decided differences. The patient recalls it positively; the parent, negatively. Most children find hospital frightening, but not Munchausen patients. They recall their early hospitalizations in glowing terms. One Munchausen patient recalled his hospitalization for a tonsillectomy at age six: "I remember it vividly. I was in this big room. Sometimes it got really dark, but that didn't bother me. The doctor picked me up and carried me into the operating room himself. When it was all over, they gave me ice cream. Lots of ice cream."

When I met the patient's mother she described the experience in totally different terms. She told me that throughout the experience her son was distraught and anxious, refused to eat or drink, and could not be controlled by her or the staff. The doctor most certainly did not carry the patient into the operating room! In the patient's mind, the hospital and doctor became nurturing replacements for a parent who had abandoned him to the hospital.

These distorted reports of abuse and romanticization of childhood hospitalization also lay the groundwork for a lifetime pattern of factitious reporting.

Often, the Munchausen has observed genuine illness in a family member or friend that predates his feigning illness. It may have provided the first opportunity to observe how much attention is paid to sick individuals. Presenting his medical history, one patient told me he had a sister who had a life-threatening asthma attack and that, not long after, he started wheezing and choking, was rushed to the hospital and given his first chance to observe doctors at close hand.

Psychiatrists who have listened carefully to Munchausen patients' histories often detect parental attitudes toward illness that are similar to those found in many cases of somatization disorders. That is, one or both parents are revealed to have been sickly or hypochondriacal and required excessive care, affection, and attention. The child observing this develops the idea that being sick has its rewards.

One of the more confounding aspects of Munchausen syndrome is the patient's astounding tolerance for pain. On more than one occasion, Munchausen patients have been likened to Sufi Moslems and other fakirs who walk on coals and lie on beds of nails. This may be inborn; but it also may result from an ability to achieve trancelike or meditative states that raise the pain threshold. Why this is so, we just don't know.

Finally, a discussion of Munchausen syndrome must include the patients' involvement with death. Munchausen patients do not talk about death, although they approach the end with frightening regularity. Perhaps they feel they have the power to forestall this horror because of a grandiose sense that they can control everything in their lives, death included. One patient stays in my mind because she defied death for so long. Mrs. Q. was thirty-five and weighed thirty-six pounds when she was admitted to the hospital. The registered nurse who had cared for her at home for fifteen years sat outside her hospital room zealously guarding her. Curled up in bed, Mrs. Q. reminded me of the wizened premature infants one sees in neonatal nurseries. She complained of constant pain and, indeed, her fragile bones, the result of malnutrition, were broken in a number of places. She had starved herself many times before, and her hospital record showed that she had innumerable admissions for other self-inflicted illnesses. This time her doctors were not optimistic about her prognosis.

Mrs. Q. spoke openly of death when I asked her how it felt to be so close to the end. She said that she often tested death; she wanted to know what it would feel like to be dead and then revived. I also learned that she had once volunteered to wash dead patients' bodies, and she described the fulfillment that working with corpses brought her. I knew she had entered into a delirious state many times. To her, the delirium felt like death. Delirium is often seen in people approaching death and is thought to spare us the final agonies. This time, however, she had been too much of a tease; shortly after our meeting, she died.

Thus far, I have provided snapshot portraits of some of the Munchausen patients I have encountered. Indeed, most of the Munchausen patients we see allow us no more than a snapshot now and then. The next two chapters tell the stories of patients who did not discharge me as soon as they learned I was a psychiatrist but allowed me the luxury of a few visits and, occasionally, the opportunity for a family meeting. Although they granted me only limited rights to explore their emotions, they did allow me to gain some insight into the illness itself. The story of

Kathy Ryan is an anomaly—the story of a Munchausen patient in whose history I was able to share, because, by chance, she became a patient of a colleague who was also a close friend and who turned to me for assistance. The remaining case histories are more representative of the illness.

·12·

Physician, Hurt Thyself

Dr. Lanie Mansel, a colleague whom I had known since our residency days, lived and practiced in Chicago. I was there for a psychiatric convention one May, and we caught up with each other on an early-morning jog along Lake Shore Drive. After running for a while, she asked me if I would offer my opinion on a patient she'd been seeing who was proving extremely difficult to treat, a young woman with both psychological and medical problems. "Just up your alley," Mansel said. I was flattered by her request, not knowing at that point I had once seen this patient. I agreed to meet her the following day in her downtown office.

The next morning, Dr. Mansel told me that the case she was struggling with involved a twenty-five-year-old medical student who had been in therapy with her for two and one-half years. This young woman had a life history of medical illness and dozens of hospitalizations, but it was her marital problems that had originally brought her to Dr. Mansel's office. Dr. Mansel, respecting the rules of confidentiality, did not reveal her patient's name, but briefly into the history, I interrupted and said, "You're talking about Kathy Ryan." Years had passed since I had met Kathy, yet I immediately recognized her as the person who was giving Dr. Mansel extraordinary cause for concern.

"Do you remember her?" Mansel asked.

"Yes. Ten years ago, I saw her a few times in consultation at the hospital."

"Do you remember your diagnosis?"

I thought for a moment. "At the time, I think I saw her only as a difficult patient."

Dr. Mansel smiled. "I knew you had seen her, but I wasn't sure you would remember her. You see, as part of her treatment, she allowed me to write for her hospital charts. And I've met her parents."

I felt embarrassed, remembering how little I had contributed to the understanding of this patient at the time. "Yes," I said, "but she made such an impression that as I became more involved with these mind/body problems, I reflected back on her case and came to some interesting conclusions. But finish telling me your part of the story first."

Dr. Mansel began by giving me the parents' version of the patient's history. Kathy Ryan was the youngest of three children. Her parents recalled a normal, healthy childhood until about midyear in the second grade. Then, suddenly, Kathy developed serious illness. Her distraught parents blamed themselves because, for two years, they had directed all their resources toward Kathy's older sister, Nora, who had been diagnosed as having ulcerative colitis. Ulcerative colitis is a debilitating, energy-sapping disease. The patient has ulcers in the colon, constant bouts of diarrhea mixed with blood and mucus, and acute pain. The patient suffers considerable humiliation, and the prospects for recovery without major surgery are not good.

Nora, who was seven when she had her first symptoms, had been fighting the disease for two years with remarkable courage. The Ryans, who lived in suburban Philadelphia, sought out the best physicians available, consulting specialists around the country. Family life became marked by a constant state of crisis.

At about the same time, Kathy started having behavioral problems at home and school. She refused to do the simple chores normally assigned to five-year-olds—hanging up her jacket, putting away her toys, taking her dishes from the table—and seemed to be having some learning difficulties. She became accident-prone, and her mother often received calls from the school nurse reporting that Kathy had skinned a knee or elbow in the playground.

Kathy, like her sister, complained of stomach cramps. Overwhelmed by the problems of their other child, her parents did not pay her much attention and, in fact, decided her behavior was a misguided attempt to gain attention that would best be taken care of by being ignored.

Kathy began to fight with Nora. Once, she said Nora had tried to scald her with hot water. Nora denied this and said it was Kathy who had tried to hurt her. Their parents did not know whom to believe.

After two years, Nora's physicians concluded that medical treatment had failed to stem the progress of her illness. The ulceration of the nine-year-old's colon had gotten out of hand, drug therapy had produced only minor and short-lived remissions, and her gastronenterologist referred her to a surgeon for removal of her entire colon. The family accepted this recommendation.

The week Nora entered the hospital, Kathy had a sudden attack of bloody diarrhea and cramping that lasted several days. While relieved that Nora was responding well to the surgery, the Ryans were alarmed by Kathy's condition and immediately brought her to their gastroenterologist, who confirmed the Ryans' worst fears. Kathy, too, had ulcerative colitis. She was also admitted to hospital, although not for surgery.

Kathy spent three weeks on a pediatric unit which, according to Dr. Mansel, she described with great affection. She said that the gastroenterologist there had been kind, loving, and caring. He was a god to Kathy, and the nurses were goddesses, also kind and caring, always coming to her bedside at the push of the button. She remembered little of the discomfort produced by the various procedures. On the other hand, Dr. Mansel said, Kathy's parents described this early hospitalization as hellish.

Kathy went on to experience all the symptoms of full-blown ulcerative colitis. She went to the toilet countless times each day, and the sweetened smell of her bloody stool never left the bathroom. Illness became her whole life. She had little appetite and less energy and was placed on numerous drugs; her schooling was taken care of by home tutors.

Kathy's doctors prescribed sixty milligrams a day of the powerful steroid Prednisone. This is a large dosage of a powerful steroid for an adult, let alone a child. The disease did not progress as rapidly in Kathy as it had in Nora and was marked by frequent periods of remission.

The Ryans lived in hope that a new miracle drug—one that would control the disease and not leave Kathy swollen and fat as the steroid did—would find its way to the market and she would be able to avoid surgery. Their prayers appeared to have been answered when Kathy was put on 6-mercaptopurine (6-MP), a newly developed immunosuppressive drug. Because it suppresses the immune system, its side effects were potentially more serious than those of Prednisone, but at least it did not leave Kathy physically grotesque. For a girl like Kathy, now entering adolescence, this was no small gain.

In fact, Kathy became a beautiful young woman. I remembered her as a striking blonde.

6-MP, however, did not bring the miracle that the Ryans had hoped for; by the time she was sixteen, Kathy decided that she had to have surgery. Her parents were reluctant to grant permission at first, but she quickly brought them around. Her doctors demurred. They were reluctant to perform a total colectomy, major surgery, on a sixteen-year-old. Kathy insisted, and all thirty inches of her colon were removed. Kathy then moved her bowels spontaneously into a plastic bag through a piece of ileum brought out onto her abdominal wall.

Dr. Mansel said she had learned that the hospital charts revealed that the pathologists who examined Kathy's removed colon found no evidence of ulcerative colitis, just diffuse superficial ulceration, hardly a condition to warrant such a radical procedure.

Nonetheless, colectomy cures ulcerative colitis and Kathy's physicians expected a normal and rapid recovery. However, a multitude of minor problems arose to complicate the recovery. Kathy experienced severe pain and symptoms of an obstructed bowel. Her temperature soared periodically. Her specialists presumed infection and sought its cause. Within days, Kathy reported symptoms that were not related to the surgery. She complained of pain upon urination and said she saw blood in her urine, leading her doctors to consider a diagnosis of kidney infection which would also have accounted for her fever. But her urine tests were negative.

Although her doctors felt she could be treated at home, Kathy wanted to know how her physicians could discharge her when she was still ill. Her hospital stay was prolonged and she became a demanding patient, especially in regard to her medications. The nursing staff, never doubting the extent of her pain, cossetted her and called her physicians frequently for prescriptions that increased her dosages of painkillers.

At some point during this hospital stay, one of her doctors put a question in Kathy's chart reflecting his doubts about the authenticity of her symptoms. His skepticism was not given much credence until one day, during routine temperature rounds, a nurse left Kathy, who was reclining on a heating pad, with a thermometer in her mouth for a few minutes. When the nurse returned and read the thermometer, the mercury sat at 104.2 degrees. The nurse noticed that the heating pad was no longer behind Kathy's back but next to her cheek. She suggested that they try taking Kathy's temperature again with a different thermometer. Perhaps this one was faulty or had not been shaken down properly.

Kathy became indignant; she complained that she was never left alone. The nurse, overwhelmed by the power of the patient's indignant response, backed down for the moment. When the nurse reflected on the episode and on Kathy's history in general, she realized that at those times when Kathy's fever was high, the patient had asked whoever was attending to leave the room and get things for her. The nurse both noted this in Kathy's chart and mentioned it to Kathy's physician. A close watch was instituted over Kathy. She was not left alone with a thermometer, and the mercury never registered higher than normal. Five days later, six weeks after her admission, she was discharged.

Kathy's recovery was short-lived. A month later, her doctors readmitted her with erosive gastritis, an ulceration of the stomach wall that can result from the consumption of excessive quantities of corrosive substances such as aspirin. Her blood tests indicated a low red-cell count (anemia) and a low white-cell count. Her doctors assumed that her anemia was secondary to the erosive gastritis, which can cause considerable loss of blood through the bowels. Although the anemia was quickly taken care of with a massive blood transfusion, her white-cell count was more problematic and cause for greater concern. Unless it was the result of a preleukemic condition, which her physicians did not believe to be the case, what was it?

It was at this point that I met Kathy. Five or six days after Kathy's readmission, I was called to see the patient in consultation because she seemed so anxious. I did not find Kathy overtly anxious. Rather, she seemed confident and in command of the situation, happily ensconced in a private room overlooking a park, the television playing and a stack of romance novels on her tray table.

Kathy told me she did not need to see a psychiatrist. However, she discussed her history and current condition quite freely but from a strictly medical standpoint. I was impressed by the depth and breadth of her medical knowledge. Yet, at the end of our meeting, I realized I knew little more about the patient than when I had knocked on her door.

Her other physicians, however, were smarter than I was. They decided to search her hospital room and, in her bedside cabinet, found a cache of 6-MP tablets. Her gastroenterologist, angry at both himself and the patient, confronted her with the findings.

Kathy vehemently denied having taken these pills. She was indignant. So were her parents. How could anyone, least of all her physicians, imply that Kathy was medicating herself with immunosuppressive drugs to deliberately lower her red and white blood cell counts? However, as with the thermometer incident, once the pills were confiscated, Kathy's blood counts returned to normal.

As Dr. Mansel paused before turning to her own first encounter with Kathy, I recalled that these events had left an indelible impression on me, although I did not grasp their implications. At the time, I could not make complete intellectual or psychiatric sense of what was happening. The notion of a beautiful young adolescent, cool and collected in the face of serious illness, creating her own sickness was alien to me. In fact, rather than making what now seems like an obvious diagnosis, I had played with the idea that Kathy Ryan was malingering. Malingerers feign illness with a specific purpose in mind. For example, a worker who wants to collect disability payments may pretend to have chronic back pain, or a drug addict, seeking a clean bed and hot meals, may feign symptoms of physical or psychological illness and manipulate a hospital admission. But such individuals do not do what Kathy Ryan did, that is, continuously feign symptoms and create physical illness as part of her life-style.

Dr. Mansel went on to tell me that when Kathy began treatment she was a newly married, second-year medical student who was having marital problems. Her young husband had not been able to cope with her many illnesses. They both came to the first few sessions, and each gave a history of the marriage; their versions varied only in minor details. What Dr. Mansel learned was that Kathy's husband had withdrawn from his wife sexually.

Dr. Mansel originally thought that Kathy's husband, Larry, would become her patient. Larry Corchoran (Kathy used her maiden name) appeared to be an affable, intelligent, reasonable young man intent upon making their marriage work. Kathy, on the other hand, made a more striking impression on Dr. Mansel. "What I noticed even more than her physical presence, and she is quite beautiful, was her strength. She had an iron will and, no matter what, we always discussed what she wanted to discuss."

By the end of the third session, Dr. Mansel said that she was fully versed in Kathy's medical history. Since I had met her, Kathy had repeated bouts of gastritis, several urinary tract infections, frequent hospital admissions for blockages in her ileostomy (surgical exit of gut on the abdominal wall), migraine headaches, fatigue and bed rest subsequent to anemia, a miscarriage, frequent and unexplained vaginal bleeding that had been diagnosed as a rare form of endometriosis, and minor surgery for another, unrelated gynecological problem. She told Dr. Mansel that she had undergone fourteen hospitalizations.

In the ensuing sessions, Dr. Mansel continued to admire Kathy's strength but also sensed an undercurrent of martyrdom. Kathy's whole identity seemed to be tied to her being sick. All her talk of illness made Dr. Mansel apprehensive. Dr. Mansel also wanted to touch on different aspects of her personality and establish some other form of contact with the patient. But Kathy gave no sense of wanting to move in other directions. The conversation always reverted to medical matters—Kathy's. Dr. Mansel said she noticed that Larry listened to his wife's recitation with obvious weariness, and she felt that their relationship was more troubled than either was letting on.

At the same time, Lanie Mansel said she noticed that she was feeling angry at Kathy. Just as patients transfer feelings of love and hate, experienced originally for parents, onto their psychiatrist, psychiatrists may experience emotions with regard to the patient inappropriate to their relationship. This is called countertransference. It muddies the psychiatric waters, and a good psychiatrist begins to analyze such emotions as soon as she notices them. I knew Lanie well; she was a good psychiatrist, but in this case she could not identify the source of her anger or entirely rid herself of it.

Kathy Ryan told Dr. Mansel that she had seen a psychiatrist a year or two before, and she gave Dr. Mansel permission to discuss her case with him. When Dr. Mansel spoke to this psychiatrist, Dr. Hood, he told her that after six months of treating Kathy, he concluded she was feigning illness. Dr. Mansel was taken aback and asked how Kathy had reacted to this idea. Hood said that he had never gotten the chance to tell her, because as soon as he realized what she was doing, she left treatment. He could only conclude that "the young lady had marvelous antennae."

Dr. Mansel's feelings were polarized. She was not convinced that Dr. Hood's interpretation was sound and was reluctant to consider that Kathy was feigning illness. Yet this possibility began to nag at her. She had a session with Larry, who came alone to the office because Kathy had heavy vaginal bleeding and was bedridden.

Dr. Mansel decided to change the direction of the therapy. Up to this point, she had been doing her best to be supportive of the couple. She hoped to help them find a rational basis for the continuation of their marriage—"to teach them to be kind to each other." But, by now, it was clear that this plan had failed. For one thing, Kathy dominated the couple's therapy. Dr. Mansel said she felt as if she were at the center of a power struggle that Kathy was always winning.

Dr. Mansel decided it would be better to try to help Larry deal with his sexual problems. She suspected that his withdrawal was caused by his anger. She wanted to make him recognize this anger and express it, knowing that he had considerable pent-up resentment at the way his wife was controlling him through her illnesses. At this solo meeting, Dr. Mansel learned that Larry had been a jogger and skier but had given these up because Kathy disapproved—and required so much care and attention.

I listened carefully to Dr. Mansel. I suspected that she, too, had suffered feelings of frustration. Clearly, she was more comfortable with not having to deal directly with Kathy. Because Lanie Mansel is a highly skilled psychoanalyst who is used to helping her patients gain insights into themselves, I surmised that the vague and unaccountable sense of anger she felt toward Kathy sprang from her own feelings of impotence.

She said she continued to work with Kathy's husband and thought he was making progress. After three or four sessions with him, however, Kathy rejoined the treatment, and Larry came less frequently and soon not at all. Little was said about his defection, and Kathy's individual therapy continued.

Months passed and Dr. Mansel, doing what a psychiatrist does best, listened. She realized that her patient was full of resentment, capable of astonishing self-centeredness, and absolutely fixated on her own body.

Quite unexpectedly, about ten months into therapy, Kathy, not permitted to write prescriptions as a medical student, forged a doctor's signature on one and was caught. Called to the dean of the medical school's office and told to explain her behavior, Kathy said she had been raped and, in the emotional wake of the attack, decided she needed tranquilizers. Sympathetic to the young woman's plight, the dean dismissed her with a mild reprimand.

Kathy gave Dr. Mansel an explicit description of her rape. She told how the rapist abused her physically and mocked her as freak when he discovered her ileostomy. Lanie Mansel told me that Kathy's description made her feel uneasy.

Soon after, Kathy reported that a fellow student had made sexual advances toward her and this had depressed her. Dr. Mansel, a woman of strict sexual morality in her own life, was protective of her patient. She suggested ways of dealing with the man. Kathy seemed comforted, but, after the session, Lanie Mansel realized that she did not believe Kathy's story—not a word of it. It sounded rehearsed and too full of circumstantial detail. This was not the first time that Dr. Mansel had heard tales of sexual overtures; Kathy Ryan's was different. Now, Lanie Mansel also questioned the rape story.

Dr. Mansel began to ask herself what she was doing for this patient. She believed that Kathy was a sick woman. But could she be helped, and was she the doctor to help her? Psychotherapy requires mutual honesty to be effective. Dr. Mansel was now convinced that this requirement was not being met by Kathy. Yet she also knew that an open confrontation with Kathy would mean the end of the treatment.

"What is the point of being a psychiatrist if you can't help people like this?" my friend asked.

I realized how intensely she related to Kathy's problems, but I did not have the answer to her question.

"I kept coming back to what Dr. Hood had told me," she said. "I knew there were patients who manufactured illnesses, but I could not accept this of Kathy. Nonetheless, I decided to check whether anyone else shared my suspicions or had a similar reaction to her." She called the patient's gynecologist and asked whether Kathy might have a factitious disorder. The gynecologist said "categorically not" and told Dr. Mansel her condition was "unique." Dr. Mansel continued, "I asked what he meant by 'unique,' and he gave me a long explanation and what I could only take to be a cockamamie diagnosis. Whatever the cause of Kathy's vaginal bleeding, this gynecologist had not found it."

Dr. Mansel said that Kathy began to cancel her sessions, always giving illness as a reason. She said her vaginal bleeding had increased and she was exhausted and in pain. She said it was taking superhuman efforts to keep up with medical school.

Kathy's absence did not mean that she left Lanie Mansel's thoughts. Her therapist often wondered what Kathy wanted from treatment. It could not have been a cure, Dr. Mansel knew with intuitive certainty. Could it be only another venue where she could retell her medical history and recite her catalogue of grievances?

Some months later, Kathy called, demanding an immediate appointment. Dr. Mansel obliged. "She came in looking like death itself. Her hematocrit [red blood cell count] must have been about two [forty is normal]. I was overwhelmed with pity and curiosity."

At this impromptu session, Kathy talked reflectively about herself, her illnesses, and the demands they placed on her energy. Quite dramatically, feeling herself drawn into a bizarre game of charades, Dr. Mansel told her how courageous she thought she was, pursuing her difficult studies in the face of such adversity. She knew that Kathy was entirely sincere when she spoke of herself as a sick person, and she even contemplated confronting the patient with her ideas. She thought better of this, feeling that it would be of no value. Instead, she suggested rather feebly, "There are elements of your behavior that may contribute to your illness."

Characteristically, Kathy interpreted this to mean that her dogged efforts to deal with life had overtaxed her. When she rose to leave, Dr. Mansel took her arm, brought her downstairs, and personally put her in a taxi. It was a gesture she would not normally have allowed herself.

Two weeks later, Dr. Mansel received a phone call from the psychiatrist to whom she had referred Kathy's husband. "Kathy Ryan must be having an affair," he told Dr. Mansel, who discredited this notion as absurd. Dr. Mansel now knew Kathy was too smitten with disease to have any other love.

Six months later, Kathy arrived at a session and proclaimed that she was pregnant. A glance at her abdomen bulging out of her slim skirt seemed to confirm this diagnosis. She also announced that she was dropping out of medical school. "I'd rather raise kids than be a physician."

Lanie Mansel, herself a mother who had been torn at one point between caring for her children and developing her practice, was touched. She was also struck by Kathy's description of her physical condition. The pregnancy notwithstanding, she had no appetite, had lost weight, and still reported vaginal bleeding. The young woman Dr. Mansel had known when their relationship began seemed to have aged. Her hair was dull, and sharp lines of pain were set around her eyes and mouth. Something else struck Dr. Mansel, too. If Kathy's life revolved around illness (by now, my colleague was persuaded that Kathy *was* creating these illnesses), how could she become a mother? She found it difficult to imagine Kathy bearing life. The psychiatrist found it even harder to imagine Kathy in the nurturing role.

Dr. Mansel congratulated her patient at this session but afterward did an extensive review of the charts she had been allowed to requisition and the notes she had taken during their sessions. Whatever explanation she was looking for, she could not yet find.

Several months later, Lanie Mansel received a birth announcement. Kathy Ryan Corchoran had given birth to a six-pound girl. Dr. Mansel was suddenly alarmed by an idea that this mother might be inclined to harm her baby. She contacted a lawyer who specialized in psychiatric problems and asked if she should contact Larry and share her fears. The lawyer said that Mansel's suspicions were of no legal significance. As for any ethical considerations, she must decide for herself. Lanie Mansel made no phone calls.

After the birth of her child, Kathy returned to Dr. Mansel's office for what turned out to be a final visit. She had moved to Evanston, completed her medical degree, but postponed her internship to stay home with her daughter. Her health had not improved much. She still had chronic anemia, gynecological difficulties, occasional bouts of gastritis, and frequent migraine headaches. Then ten days before Lanie Mansel and I met, she had received a call from Kathy's distraught husband. Kathy, he said, had tested HIV positive.

Saddened, Dr. Mansel was not entirely shocked. How many blood transfusions and invasive procedures had Kathy had over the past ten years? They certainly could have put her at risk.

This was the end of Lanie Mansel's part of the Kathy Ryan story. Could she have been wrong, she asked me, suspecting Kathy of manufacturing her symptoms, of creating illness?

I did not think so. By this time, I knew what the diagnosis was. I shared my conclusion with Lanie. I received confirmation just days later when Lanie called to say she had learned through the grapevine that Kathy Ryan was not HIV positive. Yes, her blood, for reasons that were unclear, had been screened for AIDS. But when the results came back negative, she had lied to her husband.

Kathy Ryan was a classic case of Munchausen syndrome.

·13·

Medical Terrorists

Munchausen patients are the terrorists of the medical world. Playing by their own rules, they subvert their care, strain the resources of the medical system to the breaking point, frustrate the doctor-patient relationship at every turn, and spread anarchy on hospital wards. Initially sympathetic to their plight, physicians invariably become guarded and even alienated. But faithful to the Hippocratic oath, humanitarians at heart, and respectful of the rule of law, doctors are always willing to reopen a case or renegotiate a relationship. Nonetheless, Munchausen patients manage to slip through established borders, thwarting attempts to arrive at treatment and rendering their illness "incurable."

THE HAND THAT ROCKS THE CRADLE

I learned about Pam from a pediatrician colleague who felt that the case would be of more than routine interest to me.

Pam weighed eight pounds, two ounces when she was born. The fourth child of a thirty-five-year-old mother and forty-two-year-old father, she was a full-term baby and her delivery was normal. Everyone remarked how well formed Pam was at birth, how her higher birth weight made her look more developed than most newborns, and how rosy cheeked she was.

Her healthy mien was soon to fade. Pam did not gain weight as she should have. Her mother, who was nursing, said that the baby had trouble finding the nipple and did not suck adequately. In pediatric parlance, she was a poor nippler. Her mother said also that Pam was difficult to schedule, often refusing to awaken when her mother wanted to nurse her.

When she was two weeks old, Pam suddenly turned blue when she was nursing. Her parents rushed her to the emergency room, where it was thought she had choked and had some brain damage. But an electroencephalogram and a CAT scan of the abdomen and head were normal. When a tube with a manometer was inserted to measure her stomach contractions, Pam's physicians noted an increased tendency to regurgitate and bring up too much of what she had swallowed. If some of the regurgitated matter entered the respiratory system through the trachea, the baby would choke and turn blue.

Pam was taken off the breast and started on formula. Her mother was instructed to hold her in an upright position when she fed her. This new regimen made no difference. Pam was not gaining weight. She had what is known as a "failure to thrive," or FTT. It is a symptom and sign of many childhood diseases.

It was not surprising that Pam's intelligent, experienced, and concerned mother brought her to another pediatrician. The mother told the pediatrician that Pam was spitting up the formula and not having bowel movements. Upon hearing this and noting the child's failure to thrive, the doctor arranged for Pam's admission to another hospital. Refusing to leave her child's crib, sleeping in the room, the mother was taught to feed the infant through a tube inserted into her stomach. More tests were done, this time to test whether the child had a failure of her absorption systems. These results were negative. Her mother claimed that the reflux of food from the baby's stomach continued, and two powerful drugs were prescribed.

At four months, Pam weighed less than nine pounds and was admitted by yet another pediatrician to yet another hospital. Again, her mother remained in her child's room around the clock. Not surprisingly, she struck up friendships with the resident staff, who did not fail to note in Pam's charts how pleasant and medically knowledgable her mother was. One noted that the mother said she had once worked as a baby nurse.

During this period, massive investigative procedures were pursued. Many pediatric specialists were consulted. One suggested that a catheter be surgically placed in the baby's neck vein through which she could be fed intravenously. This was done; the next day, Pam's mother told a nurse that she had dreamed the catheter had come out. "Would someone please check it?" she asked. Sensitive to the mother's anxiety, the nurse did just that and, indeed, discovered that the bulb at the end of the catheter that was supposed to keep the tube in the vein was lying outside the wound. This was strange because the dressings appeared undisturbed. The catheter was reinserted.

Next, the baby's temperature dropped to ninety-five degrees. Pam's doctors attributed the hypothermia to sepsis caused by the intravenous catheter. Because this was the only way she could be safely fed, they replaced the catheter with a new sterilized one.

Despite their fondness for the distraught mother, the nursing staff became suspicious. They began to watch mother and child more closely. They noticed that although the mother was with Pam all the time, her interactions with her daughter were minimal. They drew no conclusions from this behavior at the time.

The mother then reported that the baby would not take a bottle—added as part of an all-out effort to nourish the child—and the nurses discovered that it was filled with ice-cold formula. No infant takes readily to cold fluids, and the staff knew that the bottle had not been given to the mother at that temperature. In those moments when the mother left Pam's cribside, the nursing staff began to feed her baby themselves. They had no difficulty. Pam was an eager eater and a virtually burpless baby.

When Pam's mother realized that the nurses were feeding her child, she became enraged. Her mood turned from pleasant to dark, sarcastic, and menacing. "Why do I need to be watched putting formula in a bottle? Do you think I'm doing something wrong?" she asked intimidatingly.

One evening, a night nurse noticed the mother emptying a bottle into the child's blanket. When the mother brought the soiled blanket to the nurse's attention, she said that Pam had thrown up her last feeding.

At this point, the staff realized that they had never met the baby's father. Surely, he must be distraught. He was asked to come to the hospital. When confronted with the possibility that his wife had lied about the baby's symptoms and had simply not been feeding her, he became enraged and told the staff that they were making up stories. After all, he had three other healthy children at home.

Undaunted, the nursing staff ignored the mother's protests and took charge of Pam's care and feeding. The child began to gain weight and thrive. Charges of child abuse were brought against the parents; when the time came for the infant's discharge, social services placed the child in foster care.

My colleague was correct when he said that I would be interested in this case. Pam's condition is called Munchausen by proxy. It is caused by parents who fabricate symptoms in their children by injuring them and motivate physicians to perform extensive medical procedures.

Munchausen-by-proxy mothers have been known to simulate bleeding, neurological abnormalities, rashes, fevers, and abnormal urine in their offspring. They have no qualms about adding their own blood to their children's urine, feces, or vomitus samples. They heat thermometers, add chemicals to blood samples, administer tranquilizers and sedatives in large doses (thereby producing neurological symptoms), and apply pressure to their children's necks to induce seizures.

Nine percent of the affected infants and toddlers die; 75 percent suffer terrible side effects. Doctors have attributed some cases of sudden infant death syndrome (SIDS) to Munchausen by proxy, the mothers having smothered their children to death. Sometimes a mother carries her infant, blue from lack of oxygen but still alive, into the emergency room claiming SIDS.

Fathers are rarely reported as perpetrators. In most instances, the mother abuses the child and the father stands by, aloof and incredulous.

These infants endure this treatment for an average of thirteen months before their mothers' behavior is detected and exposed.

In part, this is because the mothers escape detection by going from doctor to doctor, and hospital to hospital. They supply their children's false medical history with cunning, dexterity, and apparent sincerity. Many are doctor's secretaries, nurses, or medical aides and technicians; some are themselves Munchausen patients.

The babies are often the recipients of the procedures their mothers crave for themselves. This suggests that they cannot distinguish between themselves and their children, a failure of definition commonly observed in Munchausen patients.

If the mothers do not have Munchausen syndrome, they usually have a history of unusual body awareness, fear of disease, or dependence on physicians for solace. According to one researcher, these women often have family members who are chronic somatizers.

Ultimately, the greatest harm to these children is inadvertently done by physicians who see little recourse but to pursue diagnoses with invasive procedures. Roy Meadow, the pediatrician who first identified and named Munchausen by proxy, wrote: "Doctors have stereotyped ways—a symptom or sign is matched by an investigation or treatment. We still behave as if missing an organic cause for a complaint is the greatest sin. It is not. It is far worse to batter a child to near death with investigations and treatment when the problem is the mother's behavior."

THE MAN WITHOUT A SHADOW

Rich Williams, thirty-two years old, said he had recently come to New York City from Phoenix, Arizona. His chart indicated that he arrived in the emergency room in a terrible state of depression. Rich told a heartrending story of the loss of his wife to leukemia four months before, followed by a period of despondency. He could not sleep and was unable to make decisions. He had decided to "get away from it all" and start life afresh in New York City.

Upon arriving in Manhattan, Rich was held up at gunpoint and robbed of all his money. He spent that night at a police precinct house, because he had no one to wire him money for a ticket back home. Rather than contacting the Travelers Aid Society, Rich, who had been diabetic since childhood, now desperate, overdosed on insulin. He was found unconscious in the men's room of a fashionable hotel and admitted to a hospital across town, where he developed renal colic. Rich was supposed to undergo surgery for kidney stones, but he opted out and was discharged.

Rich told the doctors in the emergency room that he went to another hospital, where he was refused admission because he had no insurance. Without friends, money, or lodging, he decided to jump from a promenade along the East River. Passers-by saw him scaling the rail and alerted police, who persuaded him to let them take him to an emergency room.

Although Rich had no insurance coverage, he was in such an extreme state that a sympathetic admitting clerk, knowing there was an empty bed on the psychiatry ward, granted him admission rather than having him transferred to an overcrowded municipal hospital where he could be detained in the emergency room for days until a bed became available. The absence of medical insurance data on the front of the Munchausen patient's hospital chart is a striking finding, because patients are only admitted without this information at times of emergency. Munchausen patients dramatize their situations so convincingly, alarmed hospital staff members bypass normal procedures and admit them as emergency cases.

The ward staff took note of Rich Williams's depressed appearance and listened to the story not only of his tribulations in the big city and his wife's death, but also of his father who had died of a heart attack six years previously and his mother who had succumbed to bone cancer barely a year before. He said that his only living relative was a sister—and he was estranged from her.

Rich complained of intense pain—ostensibly from the renal colic—and his requests for painkillers were met sympathetically by a staff that knew about the acute pain of kidney stones. He kept to himself, and was seen continuously pacing his room. Because Rich had suicidal ideation coupled with an obvious depression, arrangements were made to observe him every ten minutes. He was placed on a regimen of narcotic painkillers. In addition, the nurses measured his liquid intake and urine output; they taught him to strain his urine and look for particles of kidney stones. He received insulin in the dosage he said he was accustomed to. Because he told of many admissions for ketoacidosis, a condition which indicates that diabetes is out of control, the staff monitored his urine for sugar.

Slowly and sketchily, Rich revealed more about himself. He was a keyboard player in a band. His wife, to whom he had been married for just a few years, was a beautiful woman and a well-known Phoenix psychiatrist. Her leukemia had been acute, and she died within a month of its diagnosis. Rich wept when he spoke of her. Because the patient was penniless, the staff social worker arranged for him to receive financial aid that would pay for his trip back to Arizona.

The investigation of Rich Williams's kidney stones proceeded apace. X-rays showed no stone, just a small amount of calcification. The radiologist said that this could be a stone but the odds were against it.

The patient, however, stopped collecting and straining his urine. Rich's requests for painkillers multiplied. He claimed that he was vomiting but refused to show the vomitus to the nurses. When his urine was tested before he was given his insulin, it was consistently negative for blood sugar. Moreover, his blood sugar levels were normal.

At the same time, Williams continued his furious pacing. He walked up and down the halls, loudly demanding pain medication every hour on the hour. He appealed to the other patients to tell the staff to "stop my suffering." He kept his direct dealings with the staff at a minimum.

Some of the staff began to feel that Rich was manipulating them. Others did not agree. Defending his actions in her chart note, one nurse wrote that it was understandable that he would not drink because his urine burned so badly. She believed that the amount of calcification was sufficient to explain his pain and that Rich Williams was aware of the extent of his depression and really wanted to be helped. She disparaged any possibility that he was manipulating the staff in order to receive painkillers. The staff split into opposing forces, each side having a different opinion about the authenticity of Rich Williams's symptoms and his need for pain medication.

His primary symptom was pain. Rich would say to no one in particular, "I can't stay still. They didn't give the medication I'm supposed to get. I think they are testing to see how much pain I can take." Rich Williams underwent more tests for renal stones. His psychiatric diagnosis remained constant—depression associated with a grief reaction. He refused a renal scan; he said he was in too much pain. Because Rich was not drinking, the internist began an intravenous drip. When he finally did consent to the renal scan, the results showed no abnormality. He did not have a kidney stone.

When pressed, Rich talked to the nursing staff about his grief. He was unable, he told them, to visit his wife's grave because he belonged to the Jewish tribe of "Cohen" and they were prohibited from going to grave sites. Rich said that the death of his wife had affected him much more than those of his parents.

Then his anger intensified. Rich refused to speak to the staff. He refused the painkillers. "Now you can give me the real stuff. I know this stuff was water," he said, implying that they were giving him placebos.

The social worker called other hospitals and the few telephone numbers the patient had given. It was difficult to trace Rich's previous whereabouts; he was a man of many names. The social worker verified his history by providing physical and medical descriptions and asking if they matched our Rich Williams. Her efforts bore strange fruit. No other physician felt that Rich had kidney disease or diabetes. She tried to trace Rich's Phoenix connections. No one matched his sister's description at the address he gave for her. Rich's parents had never been admitted to the hospital he named and they certainly did not die there. His wife was not listed in any directory of psychiatrists. No one with her name and illness had died at the Phoenix hospital at the time Rich gave.

One of the medical students who had been intrigued by his history confronted Rich with these lies. Rich Williams responded, "If you don't believe me, that is your problem." He added, "If I tell you my real secret, you will discharge me."

Then he gave the medical student a riddle to solve: "There is a book with my secret in it. If you can find it and bring it to me, I might tell you what it is."

The medical student was intuitive and handed the patient the *Diagnostic and Statistical Manual of Mental Disorders*. Without saying anything, Rich Williams went to the index, thumbed the pages, and stopped at the entry for Munchausen syndrome. He now told the staff that he was diagnosed as a Munchausen years ago and that he had spent almost every day of the last five years in hospitals. Rich was unable to control his lying. His symptoms always worsened on the day he was supposed to be discharged.

Williams refused to give any more personal information. The staff still did not know his true name. But he was now cheerful, having unburdened himself and revealed his true medical identity. It seemed that his name, which defined his true identity, was of no consequence; his identity could be changed at will. Rich could fabricate life's milestones and tragedies, feign symptoms, and mimic mood states whenever and however he chose. Only his medical identity was fixed, and this compelled him to simulate and create illness and live in hospitals. He could not shake this compulsion. He could give clues as to his correct diagnosis, even name it himself, but he could not alter the forces that drove him to his romance with illness. And the result was a series of broken engagements with doctors and hospitals, costly affairs underwritten by public insurance funds.

POISON GAS

Gas gangrene is an acute, severe, and painful condition that often results from bacterial infections in dirty, lacerated wounds in which the muscles and subcutaneous tissues become filled with gas and a pussy, bloody fluid with a greenish hue. Doctors often use the adjective *fulminating*—occurring suddenly and with great intensity—in their descriptions of this serious malady.

When Marie was twelve, she was admitted to the pediatric ward with this diagnosis. Naturally, Marie's physicians were concerned.

Marie's story of how she had gotten this infection in her left thigh added moral outrage to their concern. Marie told them that she came from a potato farm in Maine, where she lived with her parents and six siblings. She said her father had forced her to have sex and had torn her genitals. The tear became infected, and the pockets of air and pus had spread down the muscles and other tissues of her thigh. The pediatricians could see how this infection might occur in someone who said she often helped out in the fields.

When the doctors observed Marie's thigh, they saw air-filled swellings. When they touched the swellings, a peculiar sensation in their fingers known as crepitus confirmed the presence of air. There was also pus in the lesion. There was no trace of vaginal tearing or fever, but this did not alter their belief or dissuade them that an impropriety had taken place.

The staff was also disturbed by the presence of black, blue, yellow, and green bruises on Marie's face and arms, and when they questioned her about them, she said her parents had inflicted them on her.

The staff contacted the state department of social welfare, which verified that they were not alone in reporting Marie's parents as child abusers. The state agency added, however, that there was some doubt about the authenticity of the complaints because they had come from anonymous sources. They thought that Marie's injuries were self-inflicted.

At first, the staff ignored this information. They didn't believe Marie's parents when they denied their daughter's allegations and said Marie had withdrawn her accusations of child abuse. In fact, her parents thought Marie should have been institutionalized. This parental attitude, coupled with their desire to have Marie confined, may have served to intensify the staff's worst fears and led them to underestimate the validity of much of the other information they had gathered.

Marie told the staff that she had seen her parents murder her newborn brother in some mysterious religious rite. She had been sworn to secrecy, she said. Her parents were powerful; they kept questioning her, wanting to know whether she had spoken to anyone about how she had gotten into her present condition. Marie said that they always coerced her into confessing her behavior, good or bad.

Marie became the focus of attention and affection. Her lesions were treated with powerful antibiotics but did not improve as they should have. When she complained of constipation, the staff was ready to provide remedies. But when one nurse remarked that she had noticed Marie in the bathroom that morning and heard the passing of both stool and gas, the staff decided to confront the child.

Marie rushed to make her confession. She said that she was tired of lying about how she had gotten the gas gangrene. It was not through sexual abuse but by running in fields where thorny bushes had ripped into her flesh. She had allowed the sores to become infected.

"Why didn't you tell us?" the staff asked.

"The nurses would hate me if I told the truth," she said.

The staff social worker sought more information. I was not surprised to learn that the story of her brother's murder was pure fantasy. It seemed natural to me that her fabrications became more involved at the time of his birth. As we have seen, Munchausen patients are terribly vexed when anyone pays attention to their siblings, and their envy and anger at their brothers, sisters, and parents can become abnormally intense. Through illness, they attempt to recapture some of the affection they perceive as lost.

Marie confirmed my thinking when she shared one of her worst fears with a nurse. She said that she did not want to go home because her mother had threatened her that she was going to "get it" when she got home. Marie also said, "My mother wouldn't care if I dropped dead. All of a sudden, they care. They never cared about me at home. They only cared about my baby brother. He got all the love."

Shortly after making this confession, Marie began to vomit; but one of the nurses saw her putting her finger down her throat. By this time, the staff had become more than merely suspicious and, in an atmosphere of heightened vigilance, an aide saw Marie injecting air under her skin with a hypodermic syringe.

THE ANARCHIST

Munchausen patients are invariably colorful characters, from the clothes they wear to the words they choose to their provocative behavior. Suellen Banks proved to be no exception.

When I first saw Suellen, my eyes traveled from her feet to her hair. She wore white nurse's shoes, but everything else about her was brown. She wore brown socks, brown slacks, a brown sweater, and a big brown jacket. Her eyes were brown and, from what I could see of the wisps escaping from her brown knit ski cap, so was her hair.

Suellen was twenty-eight years old, married, and the mother of an eight-year-old daughter. She was a broad-boned woman of ample girth and somewhat unkempt. When she later took off her ski cap, I saw that her hair was unwashed and stringy. Her lips were stained bright red with lipstick that overran the boundaries of her lips. She wore no other makeup. Her cheeks were hollow, and she looked older than her years. Her size and fierce look unequivocally said, "Don't mess with me." She confirmed my impressions when she looked me straight in the eye and said, "Rules are meant to be broken."

Suellen arrived on the psychiatric ward with four suitcases that were toted by a perplexed cab driver, whom she quickly paid and dismissed with an "Off with you, buster" that evoked scenes from old Hollywood movies.

One rule on a psychiatric ward that cannot be broken requires that the contents of patients' suitcases be inspected for reasons of personal safety. Suellen was not happy with this, told us so in unprintable language, and stood by, seething with hostility, as the nurses looked into her bags. Two were filled with books whose titles—*The Blessings of Marriage, In Times of Sorrow, I Want Happiness Now, When Love Seeks, There Is a Place Where You Are Not Alone, I Need Love, Fully Human, Fully Alive*—rather pathetically reflected a sense of loss and longing, a desire for love, nurturing, and life. I wanted to believe they suggested a romantic soul beneath a crude and formidable exterior.

The balance of her luggage held a full wardrobe, including forty pairs of pink nylon panties (some with holes), pink nightgowns, and numerous pairs of brown slacks and socks and sweaters. She also had household gadgets, a Walkman, three alarm clocks, and several pouches filled with cosmetics. I realized that I was seeing all of this woman's worldly possessions. The inspection over, Suellen lost no time in challenging the staff with a recitation of her medical credentials. She told us that she had been a medical secretary, paramedic, baby nurse, hospital clerk, and nurse's aide.

Suellen was admitted to the psychiatric ward because she had been taking large doses of narcotic painkilling drugs. Her physician wanted them to be slowly withdrawn under hospital supervision. When she told me just how much and many drugs she had been taking, I marveled that she was even alive. She said they were all for pain, overwhelming pain that was the result of severe stomach, kidney, and lung diseases. Suellen also was on other medications, including high doses of Prednisone (prescribed for a condition she called idiopathic pulmonary fibrosis), three antibiotics, Urecholine (in doses ten times those normally prescribed for difficulty in urinating), and Dalmane at four times the normal dosage for sleep. She said that she had been taking these and other drugs for about ten years. She kept them in a toiletries bag that we later learned she had hidden in her coat lining and then hidden in the locker drawer next to her bed.

The patient's history of medical illness dated to her early twenties, when she had had pulmonary problems that restricted her breathing. Suellen visited many famous clinics and specialists to learn the cause of her illness. Just a few months ago, she told us, physicians at a famed midwestern hospital had come up with an answer. They said that her lungs were scarred and prescribed steroids, which she said helped somewhat, "but only somewhat."

Over time, Suellen's physicians had become loath to prescribe so many painkillers, and she had to obtain them through different channels. "It's a good thing I work in the field," she said. "I have friends who can get me any medicine I want. Yes, any drug. Doctors are so uncaring, I have to go to other sources."

I found myself unable to empathize with this patient, despite a medical history that should have evoked considerable feeling. Although she described her diagnoses in detail, she was sketchy when it came to her actual symptoms and appeared less concerned than I would have expected from someone suffering so much. On the other hand, Suellen gave her medical history with such authority, we could not find reason to doubt her. Instead, we pegged her as a haughty, arrogant, narcissistic personality with serious medical illness; we noted her flair for the dramatic.

When we discovered her store of drugs hidden in empty jars of skin cream, we confiscated them. She threatened to leave. When we did not demur, she changed her mind. Given her type of personality, I knew that we had to set limits. We also insisted on meeting her family. Again, after objections and recriminations, she relented.

Her mother, a meticulous woman with graying hair cut short and tightly permed, said that Suellen had been a problem child from the moment of her difficult, cesarean birth. Headstrong, she always got her own way. In nursery school, Suellen walked out on her teacher when she did not like something the teacher said to her. At seven, she started lying and stealing. Over the years, she was apprehended several times for shoplifting. After completing high school, she went to a two-year college, graduated as a medical technician, and always had "jobs around hospitals."

"Her medical problems started in earnest after the birth of her daughter," her mother said. "At the same time, her marriage became troubled. She was in an automobile accident about then. That's when she started complaining of the chest pains. After the accident." She added, "When Suellen's around, we fight a lot more, her dad, brother, and I."

Her brother, four years younger, clean-cut, and fit, made it obvious he had no great love for his sister. "I keep away from her," he said. "She can bluff her way though anything. She's a know-it-all."

A woman who was introduced as an old and dear family friend accompanied Suellen's mother and brother to the hospital. She proved to be a valuable resource, remembering quite a bit of Suellen's early medical history. This woman recalled that, at age four, Suellen developed fevers so high that she became delirious. "Cold baths and alcohol sponges to bring the fevers down were routine," the friend said. "Her mother was really wonderful at those times. I've never seen anyone take such good care of a child. Suellen was a handful when she was sick." She also told me that sometime in the second grade—around age seven—Suellen had a tonsillectomy. After the operation, she dressed and, without telling anyone, left the hospital, arriving home in time for dinner.

Her husband, a pleasant man, shorter than his wife and physically trim, seemed to take her hospitalizations as an unfortunate fact of their lives. "She doesn't want to be in this place," he said. "She hates doctors. Doesn't like them one bit." He told me that his wife had had seven, maybe eight, admissions to hospitals all over the place in the past year. She had undergone four hernia operations because the first three had failed. She had had treatment for polyps on her vocal cords, an appendectomy, and two ulcer operations, in addition to bronchoscopies for the lung problems and several procedures, including cystoscopy, for urinary tract complaints. He said he always cared for her when she was ill.

Suellen's husband described their marriage as one of ups and downs. She was not an easy woman to live with, healthy or sick. He said that because he himself was not in the best of health, it was easier to give in to her. He spoke about their daughter. Suellen took her to the emergency room or clinic at least twice a week when she herself was not in the hospital. "She takes real good care of her," he said. "She's a real good mother. But, really, I think Suellen makes up some of the kid's sickness. She does it to get the medicine, I think."

While Suellen's narcotic medications were being withdrawn, we spoke with her many times. We told her what we had learned from her family and friend. Suellen was nonplussed by it all. Then she developed new abdominal pain and demanded that we reverse her treatment and give her back her painkillers. At the same time, her pain did not deter her from instigating a mild rebellion on the ward. She had an acute instinct for ferreting out paranoid patients and convincing them that the staff was not interested in their welfare. When we learned of these activities and confronted Suellen, she just shrugged her shoulders and muttered expletives under her breath.

Next, Suellen lived up to her initial threat and began breaking the ward rules. She smoked in rooms where there were oxygen tanks, turned up the television full blast in the lounge late at night and early in the morning, and directed harangues full of vitriol and vile language at staff members.

One day, a nurse found Suellen in the bathroom, vomiting profusely. Her vomit was an alarming dark brown and fecal smelling. The brown vomitus covered most of the bright red lipstick that ringed Suellen's mouth.

She begged for pain medication, saying she had so little stomach left. "Where is your pity?" she implored. Hysterically, she told us the precise names of the surgical procedures that had carved up her stomach: Billroth I and Billroth II gastrectomies. I could not help but be impressed by her medical knowledge. I had by now long forgotten the old, autocratic Viennese surgeon Christian Albert Theodor Billroth, who first did gastrectomies in the nineteenth century.

I must admit that despite all the history I had gotten from both patient and family, and the clues the patient had dropped, my thoughts did not run to Munchausen syndrome. The realization that my memory of surgical procedures had dimmed over the years brought me to heel and reminded me that I am, after all, an M.D.

I continued to entertain diagnoses of medical illness, although this was not strictly my responsibility, since a very capable internist was attached to the unit. But, of course, forcing oneself to think of every medical possibility is what a physician does. Foremost in my mind at the time was the possibility of gastro-colic fistula—a tract between the colon and stomach that allows the patient to vomit fecal material. I congratulated myself for remembering this point of anatomy.

My Munchausen patient exploited this vanity, encouraging me to pursue this diagnosis and maintain my connection with her in this way. I was now urging our internist to investigate this condition and, not coincidentally, impressing her with my—a psychiatrist's—recall of medical and surgical conditions. I was not alone; the internist also could not resist this opportunity to track down a rare condition. And Suellen Banks seemed calm; she was inordinately appreciative of our interest in her case.

The truth about Suellen took some time to penetrate my mind. A chance observation helped speed the process when, one morning, I saw her lying quietly in bed, dressed in one of her pink nightgowns. She was not vomiting, but there were unmistakable traces of feces around her mouth. I entered her room, and the smell confirmed my suspicions. I saw brown marks on her fingers and under her nails. It was clear that she had been eating her own feces to induce vomiting.

Suellen's game was up, and she knew that we knew. She had revealed herself quite frankly. At first, she seemed eager to test us, to find out how the staff and I would respond to my discovery. But she did not have the patience. Within minutes, she had packed her four suitcases and arrayed herself once again in the brown slacks, brown sweater, brown coat, brown cap, and white shoes she had worn upon admission, repainted her lips red, and was impatiently waiting for the elevator. When last seen, she was getting into a taxi, undoubtedly ready to continue her medical adventures in another institution.

·14·

Afterthoughts . . . and Feelings

I have neither the scholar's melancholy, which is emulation; nor the musician's, which is fantastical; nor the courtier's, which is proud; nor the soldier's, which is ambitious; not the lawyer's, which is politic; nor the lady's, which is nice; nor the lover's, which is all these: but it is a melancholy of mine own, compounded of many simples, extracted from many objects, and indeed the sundry contemplation of my travels, in which my often rumination wraps me in a most humorous sadness.

> —Jaques, in William Shakespeare's
> *As You Like It,* Act IV, Scene I

Like the human spirit they investigate, psychiatrists resist being shackled. They love to wander afield. They philosophize about subjects like "humanness." They contemplate the differences between mind and brain and whether, in fact, there are any. They wonder about the existence of a soul, independent of brain and mind. Like philosophers, they affect sadness when unable to find the truth or fathom the meaning of life. Psychiatrists rhapsodize about the meaning of love; they write about it and promote it, as if it were all and nothing else mattered.

When they attend the rich and famous, a few psychiatrists (unethically) boast about their client list and, like their clients, pursue publicity. On the other hand, politically active psychiatrists pursue the rights of the downtrodden like soldiers joining battle with society. They defend their patients against zealous prosecutors and match forensic wit with lawyers.

Psychiatrists enjoy the theater; its tragedy and comedy provide a comforting contrast to the melodrama and farce of real life. In books, psychiatrists discover a refuge from a chaotic and demanding world. Viewing art, psychiatrists use adjectives like *fine, forceful, fantastic,* and, especially, *enigmatic.* Psychiatrists are moved by music and envy its composers and players who, with a facility greater than that of any psychiatrist, comfort the soul and make the spirit soar.

Psychiatrists are not above foretelling the future. Although they are notoriously poor predictors of human behavior, they persist in trying to outdo astrologers. Perhaps they enjoy divination because it gives them an opportunity to emulate philosophical scholars by creating hypotheses for no other purpose than to sharpen the mind, and be admired for it. Psychiatrists, perhaps, enjoy prediction because they secretly wish they had magical powers. Such fantasies of potency provide an emollient to the bruises they sustain in the trenches of clinical practice.

I would like to think the predictions that follow derive more from the contemplation of my psychiatric travels and simple deduction than from the position of the stars. Peering ahead, I think the number of people with somatization symptoms will increase dramatically as we enter the next century. Their individual dramas will be played out on a stage dominated by an increasingly stress-filled world and a backdrop of frequent family disruption, rapid cultural change, and advancing technology. Psychiatrists will continue to be bit players, but their utterances will reverberate behind the scenes.

Science and society have come to recognize stress as a factor in the genesis of illness. The public never seems to tire of asking questions about stress and what to do to relieve it. Group meetings to help cope are popular. All stressors are regarded as equally harmful, notwithstanding the fact that many individuals actually thrive on stress. Asked how to avoid stress during the Christmas season, a psychologist told a television audience, "Avoid doing too much; get help." Good generic advice, if not exactly profound.

Although stress is not the sole determinant of somatization symptoms, and its workings are more complicated than the television psychologist would have us believe, it does fuel and ignite somatization symptoms in the susceptible. Because many of us express ourselves physically when stressed, boosting the degree of stress may be all that is required to augment the frequency of intermittent somatization symptoms.

Major changes in the role of women are historically associated with increased somatization symptoms. In the latter part of the nineteenth century, women were the majority of sufferers of neurasthenia (a panoply of functional somatization symptoms). This condition emerged at a time when new avenues of education and professional placement were opening for women and opinions of women's role in society were being debated. This placed new stresses on women that were frequently expressed through physical symptoms. Today chronic fatigue syndrome, which shares many features in common with neurasthenia, and is commoner in women, has replaced it during a similar period of cultural upheaval.

Men are also affected by these changes. In the nineteenth century, the 10 percent of males who suffered symptoms of neurasthenia provided the illness with credibility and respectability. Overwork and excessive devotion to duty and the somatization symptoms sometimes accompanying the increased stress of industrialized America were seen as a badge of honor. Today the emphasis on financial success and the pursuit of power and status provide similar burdens and find expression in fatigue syndromes.

Besides stress, other factors conspire to fulfill my predictions. As infants, we incorporate into our minds a locket with mother's image. The portrait in the locket mirrors how we view ourselves and is of particular importance when we get into trouble. If the locket contains a picture of a mother whose presence has been stable and whose glowing smile radiates comfort, we feel good about ourselves and have a good sense of who we are. This sense of well-being and firm identity, and the possibility of taking an occasional or frequent peek at the soothing image at times of great need, enable us to monitor the magnitude of a stress in a balanced way and develop methods of dealing with it in constructive ways. If the picture in the locket is scowling, or, worse yet, our lockets are empty, or absent, we resort to other less-constructive mechanisms—such as persistent somatization symptoms—to mitigate stress and protect us from the subsequent emotional discomfort.

The cultural upheavals of the past few decades—a period of disrupted nuclear families, emphasis on the self, and changes in gender roles—have dealt nurturing a heavy blow. The children of this period are about to come of age and experience the effects. Thus, I fear a high divorce rate, family disruption, and emphasis on self will result in a greater potential for many more lockets with scowling images, lockets devoid of images, or an absence of lockets altogether. One of the effects will be an even greater prevalence of somatization. Many who have no lockets, or whose lockets contain these negative images, develop an exaggerated sense of entitlement in addition to an unstable and negative sense of self. People with these personality traits often have somatization symptoms that insulate them from chronic emotional upheaval. These features are reinforced by a society that uses victimization and history to rationalize entitlement and its aftermath—redress for past suffering.

Society has come to sanction increased attention to, and care of, the body. Body awareness is at an all-time high. Our culture revels in endeavors to prevent illness and prolong life, some medically and scientifically sound, others not. Although we cannot assume that our current preoccupation with our body and its health will cause us to have more somatization symptoms, I think that it may do so for already sensitized and susceptible people.

If my predictions of increasing somatization are valid, we will almost certainly face a rise in the costs of medical care. Even if my forecast is not in the stars, we need to contemplate the current costs of somatization in dollars and suffering. As a psychiatrist, I can only wish for more rapid psychiatric intervention. As the case histories in this book demonstrate, modern psychiatry has made considerable progress in detecting and treating many forms of somatization.

But, here, my ruminations wrap me in sadness because our society conspires against such an outcome. Our culture not only provides the basis for the increased incidence of somatization, it also continues to promote the avoidance of psychiatrists by those with somatization symptoms. Our culture perseveres in stigmatizing psychiatric illness. Culture also provides the external theories for explaining the somatization symptoms. It is easier to blame the environment than emotional upheaval. The acceptance of the emotional origins of somatization is also avoided by reducing scientific findings to a matter of opinion, as in chronic fatigue syndrome.

My pessimism is not complete; my sadness is laced with hope. A Greek philosopher said that anything pursued beyond reason turns into its opposite. The excesses of society always result in opposite, and balancing, reactions.

As for psychiatrists, some will continue to try to get on stage, even steal the limelight. The on-stage psychiatrist will try to bring the curtain down on a happy ending, but life will make this impossible.

I once foolishly informed a fifty-year-old man that I would "cure" his eighty-six-year-old depressed mother. He had never made a life apart from her and he understood that I would create a wholly different person from the exacting and overbearing mother he both loved and hated. I meant that my treatment would return her to her former self. Indeed, with medication her depression disappeared and she returned to her former self. The poor man felt devastated and, in the scene that followed, made me the butt of all his rage, unhappiness, and frustration.

A psychiatrist may understand much of a person's emotional functioning, but he cannot, and never will, comprehend it all. Nor can he achieve miracles of character transformation. The psychiatrist must be able to say "I don't know."

Psychiatrists will continue to play a part in understanding somatization, treating emotional illness, and helping people resume their lives. They will reverse somatization symptoms when they are part of a treatable associated psychiatric disorder—a major medical advance. They will mute the intensity and debility of persistent somatization symptoms. Behind the scenes, psychiatrists will research the neurochemical pathways that mediate the communication between body and mind.

As for Munchausen patients, I am neither optimistic regarding their prognosis nor am I bereft of ideas and fantasies of their treatment. Given the opportunity (unlikely), I would gather a group of Munchausen patients and provide them with a sanctuary in a medical hospital for an extended period of time. I would set them talking and telling each other their stories. I would be the group leader. I imagine there would be chaos initially as each patient tried to outwit the others. Eventually, in this protected environment, not threatened by loss, the patients might come to confront themselves and each other and recognize the true nature of their illness. Who understands a Munchausen patient better than another Munchausen patient?

Apart from helping people, psychiatrists will continue to dabble in related fields. They will try to imitate writers, artists, and particularly musicians who can arouse a depth of feeling no words can achieve. The sounds of music cannot be reproduced on this page. What a pity! Words and thoughts are products of the mind. Music, and the feelings it arouses, possesses the whole body.

Selected Sources

Introduction

Kellner, R., and Sheffield, B.F. "The One-Week Prevalence of Symptoms in Neurotic Patients and Normals." *Am J Psychiatry* 130 (1973): 102–5.

Kessel, W.I.N. "Psychiatric Morbidity in a London General Practice." *Br J Prevent Soc Med.* 14 (1960): 16–22.

Pennebaker, J.W., Burnam, M.A., Schaeffer, M.A., et al. "Lack of Control as a Determinant of Perceived Physical Symptoms." *J Pers Soc Psychol.* 35 (1977): 167–74.

Reidenberg, M.M., and Lowenthal D.T. "Adverse Non-Drug Reactions." *N Engl J Med* 279 (1968): 678–79.

The Psychiatrist as Detective

American Psychiatric Association: Diagnostic and Statistical Manual of Mental Disorders. 3d ed., rev. Washington, DC.: American Psychiatric Association, 1987.

Blashfield, R.K., and McElroy, R.A. "Ontology of Personality Disorder Categories." *Psychiatric Annals* 19 (1989): 126–31.

Fabrega H., Jr. "Psychiatric Stigma in the Classical and Medieval Period: A Review of the Literature." *Comprehensive Psychiatry* 31 (1990): 289–306.

Gelb, L.A. "Neuroscience, Psychiatry, Psychoanalysis—Crisis and Opportunity." *Journal of the Academy of Psychoanalysis* 17 (1989): 543–53.

Persaud, Rajendra D. "Psychiatry Must Become 'Post-Eclectic' in Order to Progress." *Psychiatric Times,* April 1991.

Somatization: When the Body Speaks Another Language

Kellner, R. Somatization. "Theories and Research." *J Nerv Ment Dis* 178 (1990): 150–60.

Lipowski, Z.J. Editorial. "Somatization: Medicine's Unsolved Problem." *Psychosomatics* 28 (1988): 294–97.

Functional Somatic Symptoms

Barsky, A.J., and Klerman, G.L. "Overview: Hypochondriasis, Bodily Complaints and Somatic Styles." *Am J Psychiatry* 140 (1983): 273–83.

Ford, C.V. "The Somatizing Disorders." *Psychosomatics* 27 (1986): 327–37.

Conversion Symptoms

Engel, G.L. "Conversion Symptoms." In *Signs and Symptoms: Applied Pathologic Physiology and Clinical Interpretation,* 5th ed, edited by C. M. MacBryde and R.S. Blacklow. Philadelphia: Lippincott, 1970, 650–58.

Farley, J., Woodruff, R.A. and Guze, S.B. "The Prevalence of Hysteria and Conversion Symptoms." *Br J Psychiatry* 114 (1968): 1121–25.

Fisher, S. *Body Experience in Fantasy and Behavior.* New York: Appleton-Century-Crofts, 1970.

Ford, C.V., and Folks, D.G. "Conversion Disorders: An Overview." *Psychosomatics* 26 (1983): 371–83.

Nagi, S.Z., Riley, L.E., and Newby, L.B. "A Social Epidemiology of Back Pain in a General Population." *J Chronic Dis.* 26 (1973): 769–79.

Pain

Blumer, D, and Heilbronn, M. "The Pain-Prone Disorder: A Clinical and Psychological Profile." *Psychosomatics* 22 (1981): 395–402.

Engel, G.L. "Psychogenic Pain and the Pain-Prone Patient." *Am J Med* 36 (1959): 899–917.

Lindsay, P.G., and Wyckoff, M. "The Depression-Pain Syndrome and Its Response to Antidepressants." *Psychosomatics* 22 (1981): 571–77.

Conversion Disorder and Somatization Disorder

Ford, C.V. "Somatizing Disorder." In *Helping Patients and Their Families Cope with Medical Problems*, edited by H.G. Roback. San Francisco: Jossey-Bass, 1984, 35–39.

Quill, T.E. "Somatization Disorder. One of Medicine's Blind Spots." *JAMA* 254 (1985): 3075–79.

Smith, R.C. "A Clinical Approach to the Somatizing Patient." *J Fam Practice* 21 (1985): 294–301.

Smith, G.R., Monson, R.A., and Ray, D.C. "Patients with Multiple Unexplained Symptoms. Their Characteristics, Functional Health, and Health Care Utilization." *Arch Intern Med* 146 (1986): 69–72.

Smith, R.G., Monson, R.A., and Ray, D.C. "Psychiatric Consultation in Somatization Disorder." *N Engl J Med.* 314 (1986): 1407–13.

Hypochondria

Barsky, A.J., and Klerman, G.L. "Overview: Hypochondriasis, Bodily Complaints, and Somatic Styles." *Am J Psychiatry* 140 (1983): 273–82.

Brown, J.W., Robertson, L.S., Kosa, J., et al. "A Study of General Practice in Massachusetts." *JAMA* 216 (1971): 301–6.

Gillespie, R.D. "Hypochondria: Its Definition, Nosology and Psychopathology." *Guy's Hosp.* 8 (1928): 408–60.

Kellner, R. "Functional Somatic Symptoms and Hypochondriasis." *Arch Gen Psychiatry* 42 (1985): 821–30.

Lamberts, H. "Behavioral Problems in General Practice, I: Problem Behavior in Primary Health Care." *J R Coll Gen Pract.* 29 (1979): 331–35.

Stekel, W. *Störungen des Trieb und Affektlebens: Nervöse Angst-zustände und Ihre Behandlung.* Berlin: Urban and Schwartzenberg, 1921.

Why We Somatize

Cadoret, R., Widmer, R.B., and Troughton, E.P. "Somatic Complaints: Harbinger of Depression in Primary Care." *J Affect Disord* 2 (1980): 61–70.

Cloninger, C.R. *Somatoform and Dissociative Disorders.* Philadelphia: Saunders, 1986.

Cloninger, C.R., Martin, R.L., Guze, S.B., et al. "A Prospective Follow-up and Family Study of Somatization in Men and Women." *Am J Psychiatry* 143 (1986): 873–78.

Escobar, J.I., Burnam, A., Karno, M., et al. "Somatization in the Community." *Arch Gen Psychiatry* 44 (1987): 713–18.

Escobar, J.I., Canino, G., Rubio-Stipec, M., and Bravo, M. *Am J Psychiatry* 149 (1992): 965–67.

Fenichel, O. "Defiance by Lack of Affect and the Ego and the Affects." In *The Collected Papers* (first and second series), edited by O. Fenichel. New York: Norton, 1954, 32–33.

Freedman, M.B., and Sweet, B.S. "Some Specific Features of Group Psychotherapy and Their Implications for Selection of Patients." *Int J Group Psychother.* 4 (1954): 355–68.

Grings, W.W., and Dawson, M.E. *Emotions and Bodily Responses: A Psychophysiological Approach.* New York: Academic Press, 1978.

Hough, R.L., Landsverk, J.A., Karno, M., et al. "Utilization of Health and Mental Health Services by Los Angeles Mexican Americans and Non-Hispanic Whites." *Arch Gen Psychiatry* 44 (1987): 702–9.

Karno, M., Hough, R.L., Burnam, A., et al. "Lifetime Prevalence of Specific Psychiatric Disorders Among Mexican Americans and Non-Hispanic Whites in Los Angeles." *Arch Gen Psychiatry* 44 (1987): 695–701.

Katon, W., Kleinman, A., and Rosen, G. "Depression and Somatization: A Review, Part I." *Am J Med* 72 (1982): 127–35.

Kellner, R. *Somatization and Hypochondriasis.* New York: Praeger-Greenwood, 1986.

———. "Somatization. Theories and Research." *J Nervous Mental Dis.* 178 (1990): 150–60.

Kellner, R., Simpson, G.M., and Winslow, W.W. "The Relationship of Depressive Neurosis to Anxiety and Somatic Symptoms." *Psychosomatics* 13 (1972): 358–62.

Kendler, K.S., Heath, A.C., Martin, N.G., and Eaves, L.J. "Symptoms of Anxiety and Symptoms of Depression." *Arch Gen Psychiatry* 44 (1987): 451–457.

Krystal, H. "On Some Roots of Creativity." *Psychiatric Clinics of North America* 2 (1988): 475–89.

Lesser, I.M., Ford, C.V., and Friedmann, C.T.H. "Alexithymia in Somatizing Patients." *General Hospital Psychiatry* 1 (1979): 256–61.

Marty, P., and de M'Uzan, M. "La 'pensée operatoire.'" *Rev Franc Psychanal.* 27 (suppl.) (1963): 1345.

Pilowsky, I., and Spence, N.D. "Pain, Anger and Illness Behaviour." *J Psychosom Res.* 20 (1976): 411–16.

Reusch, J. "The Infantile Personality: The Core Problem of Psychosomatic Medicine." *Psychosom Med.* 10 (1948): 134–44.

Sifneos, P.E. *Short-Term Psychotherapy and Emotional Crisis.* Cambridge, Mass.: Harvard University Press, 1972.

Tyrer, P. *The Role of Bodily Feelings in Anxiety.* London: Oxford University Press, 1976.

Warnes, H. "Alexithymia and Related States." *Psychiatr J Univ Ottawa* 13 (1988): 127–35.

Malingering

Garner, H.H. "Malingering." *Ill Med J.* 128 (1965): 318–19.

Szasz, T.S. "Malingering: Diagnosis or Social Condemnation?" *Arch Neurol Psychiatry* 76 (1956): 432–43.

Disability Syndromes

Ford, C.V. "A Type of Disability Neurosis. The 'Humpty Dumpty Syndrome.'" *Int J Psychiatry Med.* 8 (1978): 285–94.

History of Somatization

Bauer, S. *Hypochondria. Woeful Imaginings.* London: University of California Press, 1988.

Hayman, R. *Proust. A Biography.* New York: HarperCollins, 1990.

Kenyon, F.E. "Hypochondriasis. A Study of Some Historical Clinical and Social Aspects." *Br J Med Psychol.* 38 (1965): 117–33.

Painter, G. *Proust: A Biography. The Early Years* and *Proust: A Biography. The Later Years.* Boston: Little, Brown, 1959–65.

Generalized Anxiety Disorder and Obsessive Compulsive Disorder

Sheehan, D.V., Ballenger, J., and Jacobsen, G. "Treatment of Endogenous Anxiety with Phobic Hysterical and Hypochondriacal Symptoms." *Arch Gen Psychiatry* 37 (1980): 51–59.

Panic Disorder

Katon, W. "Panic Disorder and Somatization. Review of 55 Cases." *Am J Med.* 77 (1984): 101–6.

Stein, M.B. "Panic Disorder and Medical Illness." *Psychosomatics* 27 (1986): 833–40.

Monosymptomatic Delusional Disorder and Psychoses

Opjordsmoen, S. "Hypochondriacal Psychosis: A Long-Term Follow-Up." *Acta Psychiatr Scand.* 77 (1988): 587–97.

Phillips, K.A. "Body Dysmorphic Disorder: The Distress of Imagined Ugliness." *Am J Psychiatry* 148 (1991): 1138–49.

Depression

Bridges, R.N., and Godberg, D.P. "Somatic Presentation of DSM III Psychiatric Disorders in Primary Care." *J Psychosom Res.* 29 (1985): 563–69.

Hagnell, O., and Rorsman, B. "Suicide and Endogenous Depression with Somatic Symptoms in the Lundby Study." *Neuropsychobiology* 4 (1978): 180–87.

Jones, D., and Hall, S.B. "Significance of Somatic Complaints in Patients Suffering from Psychotic Depression." *Acta Psychotherapeutica* 11 (1963): 193–99.

Lipowski, Z.J. "Somatization and Depression." *Psychosomatics* 31 (1990): 13–21.

Prestidge, B.R., and Lake, C.R. "Prevalance and Recognition of Depression among Primary Care Outpatients." *J Fam Pract.* 25 (1987): 67–72.

"Some Depression Risk Factors Are Specific to Women." Report of a Press Conference held by the American Psychological Association. *Clinical Psychiatry News,* January 1991, 2.

Styron, William. *Darkness Visible. A Memoir of Madness.* New York: Random House, 1990.

Psychosomatic Illness and Psychosomatic Medicine

Bronowski, J. *Magic, Science, and Civilization.* New York: Columbia University Press, 1978.

Fawzy, I.F., Cousins, N., Fawzy, N.W., et al. "A Structured Psychiatric Intervention for Cancer Patients. I. Changes over Time in Methods of Coping and Affective Disturbance." *Archives of General Psychiatry* 47 (1990): 720–25.

Fawzy, I.F., Kemeny, M.E., Fawzy, N.W., et al. "A Structured Psychiatric Intervention for Cancer Patients. II. Changes over Time in Immunological Measures." *Archives of General Psychiatry* 47 (1990): 729–35.

Goodman, Aviel. "Organic Unity Theory: The Mind-Body Problem Revisited." *Am J Psychiatry* 148 (1991): 553–63.

Kagan, J. Snidman, N., Julia-Sellers, M, and Johnson, O. "Temperament and Allergic Symptoms." *Psychosomatic Medicine* 53 (1991): 332–40.

Kuhn, C.C. "A Spiritual Inventory of the Medically Ill Patient." *Psychiatric Medicine* 6 (1988): 87–100.

Lipowski, Z.J. "Physical Illness, the Individual and the Coping Process." *Psychiatry Med.* 1 (1988): 90–102.

Sachar, E.J., Mason, J.W., and Kolmer, H.S., Jr. "Psychoendocrine Aspects of Acute Schizophrenic Reactions." *Psychosomatic Med.* 25 (1963): 510–37.

Taylor, David C. "Hysteria, Belief, and Magic." *Int. Journal of Psychiatry* 155 (1989): 391–98.

Weiner, H. The Dynamics of the Organism: Implications of Recent Biological Thought for Psychosomatic Theory and Research. *Psychosomatic Medicine* 51 (1989): 608–35.

Weiner, H., Thaler, M., Reiser, M.F., and Mirsky, I.A. "Etiology of Duodenal Ulcer. I. Relation of Specific Psychological Characteristics to Rate of Gastric Secretion (Serum Pepsinogen)." *Psychosomatic Med.* 19 (1957): 1–10.

Munchausen Syndrome

The Adventures of Baron Münchhausen. London: Cassell, Petter, and Garpin. Undated, probably late nineteenth century.

Asher, R. "Munchausen's Syndrome." *Lancet* 260 (1951): 339–41.

Cramer, B., Gershberg, M.R., and Stern, M. "Munchausen Syndrome." *Arch Gen Psychiat.* 24 (1971): 573–78.

Cremona-Barbaro, A. "The Munchausen Syndrome and Its Symbolic Significance: An In-depth Case Analysis." *British Journal of Psychiatry* 151 (1987): 76–79.

Eisendrath, S.J. "Factitious Illness: A clarification." *Psychosomatics* 25 (1984): 110–17.

Ford, C.V. "The Munchausen Syndrome: A Report of Four New Cases and a Review of Psychodynamic Considerations." *Psychiatry in Medicine* 4 (1973): 31–45.

Frame, B., Jackson, G.M., Kleerekoper, M., Rao, D.S., DeLorenzo, A.J.D., and Garcia, M. "Acute Severe Hypercalcemia à la Munchausen." *American Journal of Medicine* 70 (1981): 316–19.

Gavin, H. *Feigned and Factitious Disease.* London: J and A Churchill, 1843.

Geracioti, T.D., Van Dyke, C., Mueller, K., and Merrin, E. "The Onset of Munchausen's Syndrome." *General Hospital Psychiatry* 9 (1987): 405–9.

Griffith, J.L. "The Family Systems of Munchausen Syndrome by Proxy." *Family Process* 27 (1988): 423–37.

Grinker, R.R. "Imposture as a Form of Mastery." *Arch Gen Psychiatry* 5 (1961): 449–52.

Hollender, M.G., Jamieson, R.C., McKee, E.A., and Roback, H.B. "Anticholinergic Delirium in a Case of Munchausen Syndrome." *Am J Psychiatry* 135 (1978): 1407–09.

Hyler, S.E., and Sussman, N. "Chronic Factitious Disorder with Physical Symptoms (The Munchausen Syndrome)." *Psychiatric Clinics of North America* 4 (1981): 365–76.

Justus, P.G., Kreutziger, S.S., and Kitchens, C. "Probing the Dynamics of Munchausen Syndrome." *Annals of Internal Medicine* 93 (1980): 120–27.

Kass, F.C. "Identification of Persons with Munchausen's Syndrome: Ethical Problems." *General Hospital Psychiatry* 7 (1985): 195–200.

Kaufman, K.L., Coury, D., Pickrel, E., and McCleery, J. "Munchausen Syndrome by Proxy: A Survey of Professionals' Knowledge." *Child Abuse and Neglect* 13 (1989): 141–47.

Lindenbaum, J. "Hemoglobin Munchausen." *JAMA* 228 (1974): 498.

Livingston, R. "Maternal Somatization Disorder and Munchausen Syndrome by Proxy." *Psychosomatics* 28 (1987): 213–17.

McDonald, J., and Wager, K. "Munchausen Syndrome Masquerading as AIDS-Induced Depression." *British Journal of Psychiatry* 154 (1989): 420–21.

Meadow, R. "Fictitious Epilepsy." *The Lancet* II (1984): 25–28.

Meadow, R. "Management of Munchausen Syndrome by Proxy." *Archives of Disease in Childhood* 60 (1985): 385–93.

Meadow, R. "Munchausen Syndrome by Proxy." *Archives of Disease in Childhood* 57 (1982): 92–98.

Mumford, M., and Tobis, J. "A Case of Munchausen Syndrome Masquerading as Unstable Angina." *Journal of the National Medical Association* 73 (1981): 661–64.

Pope, H.G., Jonas, J.M., and Jones, B. "Factitious Psychosis: Phenomenology, Family History, and Long-Term Outcome of Nine Patients." *Am J Psychiat.* 139 (1982): 1480–84.

Rosenberg, D.A. "Web of Deceit: A Literature Review of Munchausen Syndrome by Proxy." *Child Abuse and Neglect* 11 (1987): 547–63.

Shafer, N., and Shafer, R. "Factitious Diseases Including Munchausen's Syndrome." *New York Journal of Medicine,* March 1980, 594–604.

Snowdon, J., Solomons, R., and Druce, H. "Feigned Bereavement: Twelve Cases." *Brit J Psychiat.* 133 (1978): 15–19.

Spiro, H.R. "Chronic Factitious Illness." *Arch Gen Psychiat* 18 (1968): 569–79.

Stern, T.A. "Munchausen Syndrome Revisited." *Psychosomatics* 21 (1980): 329–36.

Tucker, L.E., Hayes, J.R., Viteri, A., and Liebermann, T.R. "Factitial Bleeding." *Digestive Diseases and Sciences* 24 (1979): 570–72.

Veith, I. *Hysteria: The History of a Disease.* Chicago: University of Chicago Press, 1965.

Wimberley, T. "The Making of a Munchausen." *British Journal of Medical Psychology* 54 (1981): 121–29.

Afterthoughts . . . and Feelings

Abbey, S.E., and Garfinkel, P.E. "Neurasthenia and Chronic Fatigue Syndrome: The Role of Culture in the Making of a Diagnosis." *American Journal of Psychiatry* 148 (1991): 1638–46.

Index

·D·

·E·

·F·